"The people who sat in darkness have seen a great light,

And upon those who sat in the region and shadow of death

Light has dawned."

Matthew 5:16

HE CAME LOOKING FOR ME

He Came Looking for Me is a book like none other I have read. The author's unique writing style is both captivating and refreshing. Baber masterfully parallels the experience of seeking and restoring foals once sold, to the heart of God that comes looking for those needing hope and redemption. I read it a second time in one sitting and found myself reading parts out loud to friends. You will find inspiration in the pages of this easy to read, but hard to put down book. - David M.

He Came Looking for Me is an extraordinary book that should be a must read for animal lovers. The author beautifully correlates the story of reuniting with two lost horses with the promise that God makes that He will never lose us. ... She never allows us to forget that God has a plan, and that all God asks us to do is simply move one foot forward toward that plan each day. ... Truly a wonderful book that I cannot wait to pass on to the animal lovers in my life. - Jen S.

"There are so many books in the world, and so little time to give even good books the time they deserve. There are some books, that as you read them, they are so rich, so full of imagery and truth, that you take your time trying to absorb every nuance and make your own connections. *Tess of D'Ubervilles* by Thomas Hardy and specifically two of C.S. Lewis' books (*4 Loves* and *Mere Christianity*) hold a special place in my heart as these kinds of books.

I can add Lynn Baber's book, *Amazing Grays*, to that particular book shelf. - Melinda F., *Boots and Saddles*

HE CAME LOOKING FOR ME:

A true story of hope and redemption

Lynn Baber

ISBN# 978-1-938836-04-6

Published by Ark Press

Amazing Grays Ministry, Weatherford Texas

ACKNOWLEDGEMENTS

With profound gratitude I wish to thank those who made it possible to share this message of grace and victory in Jesus Christ with you. It is the hand of God that combines events that may appear coincidental to some, but not to those who are blessed to witness His handiwork.

There are very special people with whom I enjoy herdship. God graced us all, one with the other. Where one is weak another is sure to be strong. Thank you, Baber, for every day and every year. Thank you, Barb, for being my friend, advisor, and for your help in editing this manuscript.

David Fowler, introduced me to the song, *He Came Looking for Me,* which continues to inspire me every time I listen to him sing it.

May each of you be blessed on your own journey home.

Table of Contents

PROLOGUE: DESTINED FOR SLAUGHTER

"What about this one, Daddy?" asked the pony-tailed, freckle-faced ten-year-old girl.

"He won't work for you, honey," her father replied as his eyes looked me over from my sunburned nose to my poor, short tail, and then from my sunken, thin back down to my split hooves.

Shaking his head in pity, the father continued, "Poor thing, he is a sad little man, isn't he? He has a kind eye and might have been a good horse at one time. But we need to find you a horse that is strong and healthy."

The little girl reached her small hand through the rails of the fence I was tied to and touched my face. For just a moment I touched her back. Knowing her father was right, she pulled her hand back through the fence and said to me, "I hope you find a nice home." He didn't say anything, but the father knew that probably wasn't going to happen.

The pair moved down the aisle of the auction barn away from me, our brief encounter already forgotten.

The yellow number on my thin, white hips is 83. The sale flyer describes me as a nine-year-old Appaloosa gelding. That is all. There is no mention of my name or that I was bred to be a champion.

At least there is shade here. The people brought me here early this morning and tied me to the fence. I haven't seen them since.

[11]

There have been a few people walk past me today, but not many. The only one who touched me was the little girl with the ponytail.

~ ~ ~

Bidder number two was sitting four rows up from the sale ring in-gate. He had already walked the auction pens and circled the hip numbers of the horses he figured to pick up and ship off to Mexico for slaughter.

Number 83 on his paper was circled in red.

Sitting on the wooden seat directly behind bidder number two was a man with a worn cap pulled low over his brow. He reached into his threadbare pocket and pulled out a list.

His eyes went to one of the faded, hand-written entries on the list. Each mark on the list was as familiar to the man as his own name. Knowing exactly where to look, the man's gaze settled on the name, *Signed by Sky*.

INTRODUCTION

Anna Sewell's beloved novel, *Black Beauty*, is the classic story told by a horse of a life ranging from love and service to despair and hopelessness. There are many similarities between this story and Beauty's. The main difference is that this one is true.

Within four short days in late summer 2009, my husband and I learned the absolute truth of Christ's promise that we are never alone. We were sent to find the last two foals from our Appaloosa breeding program. The events of those few days unfolded in a way only God can arrange.

The two colts were sold as the centuries advanced from the twentieth to the twenty-first. It seemed somehow fitting to begin a new program as the old millennium gave way for the new. Our Appaloosa program ended and we began to exclusively breed Quarter Horses.

It had been nearly nine years since the boys were sold. Our search was not for any Appaloosa. Our search was not for just any of our foals, but specific, by name. We needed to find Sky's last sons and bring them home.

Our search was for *Adios Cielo* (Ace) and *Signed By Sky* (Shiner).

Had we not appeared out of the sweltering heat that day in Roanoke, Shiner may have lived out the scenario established in the prologue. Based on his condition and lack of utility where else would he have gone but to a killer buyer? But Shiner's name was on the Redeemer's list and the trucks heading to the Mexican slaughterhouses had to leave without him.

- Shiner and Ace, 2000 -

He Came Looking for Me is the story of how Shiner and Ace returned home. We went looking for them. We found them. Help didn't arrive until the moment it was needed. After nine years it was needed and we showed up just in time. The hand of God is present throughout this story.

Horses have been my passion since I was four years old. God has richly blessed me by using my horses as teachers. After more than two decades as a successful equine professional I retired from the horse business. No more training. No more trophies. No more judging. No more lessons. No more foals.

[14]

Before long my life changed once again. Horses would continue to play a pivotal role in both my family and my work. The book, *Amazing Grays, Amazing Grace*, was the catalyst that morphed my horse career into a new and unexpected one. *Amazing Grays*, the book, was the beginning of Amazing Grays Ministry.

In these pages you will meet the six horses that will remain in our family until they pass through the narrow gate [Matthew 7:13] to the green pasture that waits for them beyond. When that day comes, they will again graze on lush grasses beside my beloved Sky. Sky's boys, Shiner and Ace, are the focus of this story but you will also meet my amazing grays, Bo and Swizzle, as well as Copper and Asti.

Bo assumes the leadership role when I am absent and the herd passes into his care. He is a stocky, dapple-gray Quarter Horse with the perfect disposition to be a fair and conscientious leader. Swizzle, my little powerhouse of a dark-gray filly, is as devoted to me as Bo, but in a very different way. They are amazing because through them I learned the lessons shared in *Amazing Grays, Amazing Grace*.

Copper is my husband's horse, a flashy dun gelding that attracts attention from passers-by as does our tall, elegant black mare, Asti. Each horse offers unique attributes and character to the family dynamic. We would not be complete if any were missing.

Jesus Christ promised us a mansion in heaven [John 14:2]. Our name is already on the door post. No substitutions allowed. He will come looking for us when we are most in need and bring us home.

Jesus Christ knows each of you by name, and will bring you home just in time, as we did Ace and Shiner.

"For the Son of Man has come to seek and to save that which was lost." -- Luke: 19:10

"Of those whom You gave Me I have lost none." - John 18: 9

  He Came Looking for Me isn't just the story of two horses who needed rescue. It is the story of promise and victory by relationship with Jesus Christ for each and every one of His chosen—all who have their name written in the Book of Life and engraved on a mansion door in eternity.

  He will come looking for you right when you need him most. None will be lost.

[16]

WE ONCE WERE LOST

There is a fly crawling up the inside of my left hock. For a split second I consider stomping my foot to see if it will fly away before deciding that it's really not worth the effort. My eyes are half-closed against the merciless sun of a late-Texas summer. The skin in the corners of my eyes is cracked from sunburn, something I really suffer from. Residue of dried tears from dust and sun collect in the cracks, increasing the discomfort caused by the sunburn.

I no longer notice the noise made by the fast boxes that speed to and fro on the crest of the hills that form the western boundary of the hilly, dry pasture where I live. In the darkness, the din of those big, stinky cars fades as their white and red lights flash first one way and then the other.

The first few nights after I got here, I tried to escape from the noise and lights that never seemed to end. But no matter how hard I tried, there was no place to go that the noise couldn't follow. Eventually I learned to just ignore the constant race along the top of the hills.

It is the second hot time since I came to this pasture with my brother, Ace. When we arrived there was already a small herd here. Occasionally a horse will disappear through the pasture gate, never to return. Sometimes a new one joins us here in the pasture, but we take little notice once they give

[17]

up trying to escape the noisy boxes and surrender to reality in this place.

Our Home Pasture

My brother Ace is only a few nights younger than I am. We were both born in the security of our comfortable home pasture many hot times ago. I have never known life without my brother. I often dream of that pasture and my mother, Scotch, who was always somewhere nearby. Ace's mother, Julie, was also there. While Ace and I slept, our mothers stood watch, allowing us to slumber peacefully, knowing we were protected. In those days we napped frequently, sprawled in the cool, green grass, resting up between meals and playtime. Our home pasture was wonderful, our days full and secure.

Each morning and evening the people brought all of us special food. It came in a little cart that made a funny noise as it ran around the road next to our pasture. We loved the cart and the buckets that brought exciting things to eat that were very different from the milk and grass we already knew. It was a little strange at first, but we learned to eat it with our mothers and soon began to watch for the funny little cart along with the other horses in our pasture.

My mother, Scotch, was particularly fond of the one called Lynn. Whenever my mother saw Lynn she would start off to meet her. I knew I was most special to my mother, but I know she held a special place in her heart for Lynn, too. Lynn was the first human I ever saw, right after I was born. She brought my mother and me up in to a protected little place right by the house. Lynn was with us a lot my first few days until we went back out into the pasture.

Two nights later Ace was born. We loved the attention from the people. We thought we were pretty special, the princes of the pasture. There was always something to entertain us in our pasture. We had water holes to play in, trees to scratch on, and the other horses to visit and play with.

The house where Lynn lived with the man she called Baber was less than sixty feet from the high end of the pasture. There was always something happening up there. Ace and I were entertained and the world was a wonderful place, living safely in our home pasture with our mothers.

After that first hot time, Ace and I were separated from our mothers. It was hard, but at least we still had each other. We have always had each other.

Today, Ace is somewhere down in the lowest part of the pasture trying to find a little relief from the hot Texas sun. I left the small grouping of trees to see if there might be a blade of grass somewhere that had been missed by the other horses. This pasture is large, but it's mostly dust and a few of those tall, hard weeds that are too bitter to chew.

Ace and I spent most of our lives, from one hot time to the next, very near our home pasture. We lived with a family that spent time with us and always made sure that we had clean water and food. Ace and I lived with our older brother and sister, Cielo and Snip, who moved with us from our home pasture.

Then, more than two hot seasons ago, we were brought here, Ace, Cielo, and me. Before this last hot season began, Cielo was led away through the pasture gate and never came back. None of us ever knew what happened to our sister, Snip.

[19]

The Lost Time

When we first arrived here we were confused, me especially. The humans here seemed to know Ace's and Cielo's names, but not mine. It's been a long time now since I've heard my name called. *Shiner*.

It's also been a long time since Ace and I played together in cool, green grass like we had in our home pasture. We grew up in a wooded area. This pasture has very few trees. When we first arrived, we couldn't rest because of the loud noise along the hilltop that never seemed to stop. But none of the horses seem to notice it anymore.

The only thing that changes from day to day is when the people come to get us and take us up by the buildings. We each go to a separate pen with hay and grain. Even though I am not right in with Ace, it is nice to have food all to myself, and he is next to me. After we eat, Ace and I are tied up so the humans can get on our backs. We don't go there every day, and sometimes I think I might just try to stay in the pasture…but there is food in the pens.

Ace gets scared sometimes, and mad sometimes, when the people try to ride him. I am just confused, and I get nervous when they try to take me away from Ace. The people don't seem to understand that I'm not trying to do wrong; I just need my brother. He's all I have left.

~ ~ ~

So here we are in this hot time. Neither of us is too concerned about looking for grass; we've pretty much given up on that. Ace and I go to the pens enough to keep going, though we're getting more tired and don't have the energy to play anymore, even if we should happen to think about it.

Today it is oppressively hot. My tail has gotten so bare there is no hair left to fight the flies. My coat is dried and hard where I sweated under the things they put on my back and around my belly. My feet are cracked and I am sunburned. I am sore here and there from bites and kicks where one of the other horses ran me off from the water. The skin on my tender nose is dry and peeling from sunburn, and my eyes hurt. It's just another day of the hot time.

Perhaps if I can sleep I will dream of our home pasture.

Moved Again

I was nearly asleep when the gate opens on the far side of the pasture. It is the middle of a hot afternoon and two people I don't recognize are walking down the hill into the pasture. No one is calling us, so I guess we aren't going up to the pens today.

All the other horses are spread over the pasture, each one standing alone as I am. The sun is so hot. The humans have already made their way down the first steep hill. I close my eyes again and try to sleep, hoping to dream of our home pasture.

The people are calling out. I don't know who they're calling out to, and I decide to watch them as they walk further into the pasture. I don't really care much what they're doing, but I can't seem to go to sleep anyway. The flies and the irritation of my sunburned face and back end keep me awake. I wonder what Ace is doing. Is he still down in the shade by the small water hole?

Picking their way down the rough hillside and washed places, the people seem to be coming in my direction. The two of them are close enough so I can get a good look at them and they are taking a good look at me. The smaller one quietly calls out, "Shiner?" I don't have the energy to be curious, so I am just going to stand here and wait to see what they do.

The two people move on. They stop to look at one of the other horses standing on a little ridge above me. After a bit, they continue on down a hill toward the water hole. I will try again to sleep. *Home pasture.*

~ ~ ~

The people are calling for Ace.

Eventually I see my brother slowly climb up the hill from the water hole and turn to head in my direction. The people continue calling out, "Ace!" Before long, they meet him on the dusty hillside. After speaking quietly to him for a bit they walk around him, getting close enough to pet him. I can tell he's not real sure about this. We don't get people out here much.

The people turn from Ace and start walking back in my general direction. They seem to be wandering around just a bit, but before I know it they are next to me again. I just stand as the smaller one walks around me. I'm not afraid of her, so why get excited? She takes a moment to gently stroke my shoulder. After a few moments the people set back off across the pasture and go out through the gate.

I try again to dream of our home pasture.

~ ~ ~

The next day was the same as every other, the brief visit by the people already forgotten. Ace and I lived one more day in the hot time.

~ ~ ~

The following morning we are called up to the pens. Food.

Before we finished eating one of those big moving machines pulled in near our pens. The people from the pasture get out of the machine and come over to see us. The people here and the people from the pasture sit down and talk, frequently looking over at Ace and me.

Holding a halter and rope in her hand, the small one unlatches the gate and comes into my pen. She calls softly, "Shiner." There is something familiar... After she strokes my neck and head, she hands my lead rope to the tall one she calls Baber. He starts leading me around slowly while the small one goes in to get my brother Ace.

The tall one and I watch the small one ask Ace to get up into the moving box. Ace does not like being under anything. He does not go into the box. Ace tries to pull away and come back to me so the man and I go to stand near the people here. The small one and Ace move back up to the moving box, then away. I don't understand everything they are doing, but Ace must have decided to follow her into the moving box—because he does.

What will happen to Ace? He is all I have. Will I have to go back to the dusty pasture alone, only to wait in the hot sun and try to dream?

Then the small one walks over to me, pets my head and talks to me. She keeps calling me Shiner. Once upon a time that was my name.

She leads me up to the moving box. I never was afraid of the boxes, so I get in alongside Ace. The box closes, except for the wide-open windows at our heads and tails.

At least Ace and I are still together. I widen my legs and brace against the divider as the box begins to move.

A New Day

When the box stopped moving the doors opened and the small one backed both Ace and me out. The people led us into a large pen in a place I've never been before. But as long as I am with Ace I won't get upset.

The tall one led me into a barn. I could see the far end open into to a small grassy spot and then another gate. Ace didn't want to come into the barn at first, but the tall one and I waited for him to catch up before going forward again.

We were in the kind of small dirt pasture where people ride horses, all soft dirt enclosed by a three-rail fence. The small one hung a bucket of water on the fence next to the barn. For a little while Ace and I just stood next to each other. There were horses on the other side of the fences, but I didn't pay much attention to them.

The people were doing something in the next pasture, off in the direction where the late afternoon sun is hottest. Before long, the people came back and put halters on us again. Ace tried to walk away at first, but he really didn't try all that hard, and it wasn't long before we were standing still so the tall one could look at us through a little black box he held up to his face.

Once they finished looking at us the tall one led me away again—back through the barn. I looked back quickly to be sure Ace was coming too. He was. A short walk and we went through yet another gate.

There was fresh green grass everywhere but I didn't really notice at the time. Ace was there with me. The people removed our halters, gave us a final pat and left us alone. I walked around the small pen to see if we were safe and found cool water and fresh hay. There was also feed, but neither Ace nor I had much appetite.

I found a place to stand out of the hot sun and discovered hay there too. Perhaps I would have a bite to eat after all. Ace came to stand beside me in the shade.

It has been a big day. I'm not sure what it all means, but Ace and I are still together.

There is something about the smell of the grass... She had called me by my name, *Shiner*. Perhaps I'm finally asleep and beginning to dream about our home pasture.

HE CAME LOOKING FOR ME

THE SEARCH BEGINS

Have you ever felt that something was missing in your life but had no idea on earth what it could possibly be? My husband and I were not in want of anything. What could we need that we didn't have already?

We had more than enough to do and more than enough mouths to feed. As the loving "parents" of four dogs, four cats, five horses and a donkey, we had relationships galore and were already concerned about having enough time to devote to each of them.

Did I mention children and grandchildren? We're not getting any younger, and we were already talking about the possibility that we had too many animals.

So, what in the world could be missing? An empty place had been left in both our hearts and our pastures when we lost our last Appaloosa, Sky, the previous summer to complications from total blindness. His story is told in more detail in *Amazing Grays, Amazing Grace*.

When Sky passed away our family was still large and active, and our horse relationships rewarding. Somehow, though, we felt the need for more. Somehow our family was not complete.

On a hot August evening, Baber and I sat in the house working our way through the pile of (mostly junk) mail that arrives daily. This is the time when I should let you know that my husband much prefers being referred to by his last name rather than his first. It may sound odd right now, but hopefully you'll get used to it just as I did. Okay, I was the one who started calling him Baber, and it has stuck firmly.

On this particular day the mail included the latest issue of the *Appaloosa Journal*. As lifetime members of the Appaloosa Horse Club we still receive a copy every month, though our days of placing full-page ads in every issue are long past.

After we had both finished looking over the mail I mentioned to Baber that it just didn't seem right to not have an Appaloosa in the pasture. Surprisingly, he replied that he had been thinking just the same thing. History has proven to us that when we arrive at the same place at the same time, something is afoot. Indeed, this occasion was no exception to that rule.

No Relationship Substitutions

When we lose a significant relationship in our lives no one else is ever able to fill that particular spot in our hearts. Parents who lose a child can never fill the void that remains no matter how many other children may eventually fill the house.

Research has shown that widows and widowers who enjoyed wonderful marriages are more likely to marry again, but can never replace the one lost. Each new relationship must stand on its own.

A couple of years ago I discovered that my favorite mare, Scotch Lace, had been placed for sale by the lady who bought her from us years earlier. I contacted her to get the particulars. Scotch was now a bit lame and had not produced a foal that lived till it was weaned since she left us. Scotch just seemed to have run out of usefulness from a purely market-driven point of view.

Scotch had been my favorite mare and I offered to retire her and get her off the lady's feed bill. The price she was asking was on the very high side for a mare you probably couldn't breed or ride, so I wasn't prepared to pay the asking price.

If the economy had not been on the brink of depression I might have just written a check and not cared. But things weren't looking all that good financially and we had to weigh the expense of adding one more horse to our already considerable feed bill. At the time Scotch was the only horse I would have even considered keeping as nothing more than a pasture pet. But the lady declined my offer.

In the back of my mind, I really expected the phone to ring one day and I would be told that, yes, I could bring my trailer on up and take Scotch home to live out the rest of her life with us.

That call never came. I don't know what ever happened to Scotch and I don't think I'll try to find out. Sometimes we are more blessed to not know the end of a story. Considering the events that led to this book, it seems likely that the place I was offering to Scotch already had another name on it—Shiner. In a way, Scotch sacrificed her own security so there would be a place for her last foal. She was always a wonderful mother and I can do nothing else but reckon it further evidence of the level of nobility I know she possessed.

The mansions Jesus has prepared are specifically reserved—no substitutions allowed. It seems the stalls on our place here in Texas have the same exclusivity—no substitutions. Scotch's name was not on the stall door, but there was indeed a name, and it wasn't the name of any horse already here.

~   ~   ~

Even without any Appaloosas, there were still plenty of horses on our place. Baber and I had recently been lamenting the responsibility of caring for the number of horses we already had. We're not spring chickens and most of our horses are fairly young. And again, there was that pesky economy…

> *"I have been young and now am old;*
> *Yet I have not seen the righteous forsaken,*
> *Nor his descendants begging bread.*
> *He is ever merciful, and leads;*
> *And his descendants are blessed."*
>
> *- Psalm 37:25-26*

But there was also an empty place in the family that could only be filled by one of Sky's offspring. Sky had been a National and World Champion and had sired the same. But what made him so special was who he was as an individual and what he had meant to us—to me, in particular.

We needed to bring home one of Sky's foals; nothing else would fill the empty spot in our heart. The seed began to germinate.

When God Goes to Work, Look Out!

As I mentioned earlier we have plenty to do, both at home and in the community. A week or two passed without

[30]

any further discussion about finding one of Sky's kids. It is often true that there is calm before a storm. When God is getting things all lined up we are usually blissfully unaware of all that is happening behind the scenes. Baber and I were thoroughly enjoying this rare period of uneventful routine. For most of our life together our routine has been one of non-routine.

One of my best friends and I met regularly to catch up. There is just no substitute for time spent together when building and maintaining relationships and sometimes you just need to make appointments. I was keeping one such appointment with her during the last week of August.

We were chatting at her house when it dawned on me that we had sold four of Sky's foals to an airline pilot and his family who lived just up the road from her house. It had been over nine years since we'd seen those horses, but I thought, *Well...let's go look to see if they might still be there.*

As I drove up the road I began to feel purposeful. Surely I would find the three geldings we had sold to the pilot's family and I would arrange to bring one of them home—preferably the oldest, a 1999 colt we named Clearly Cielo.

Cielo is black with a big white blanket and black spots. He looked so amazingly like his sire, Sky, that we chose this name for him, *Clearly Cielo* (which means Sky). Cielo was gorgeous and we had quite a history with him.

As a new yearling he tore a huge hole in his chest trying to get to his little friend in the next pasture. Cielo reared up to get across the fence and come down on the top of a t-post, tearing his chest open from the bottom left all the way across to the top right.

[31]

Cielo was out in the middle of one of the large front pastures when Baber looked at him and noticed something odd. From a distance we didn't really see anything but Cielo just standing still, looking somehow wrong. To be on the safe side we headed out into the pasture to investigate.

My heart probably missed a beat or two when I saw what had happened. There wasn't even much blood, just jagged, shredded skin and hide dangling below Cielo's neck. Baber went for the truck and trailer. I put a halter on Sugar, Cielo's grandmother and led her up to the gate by the house. Cielo followed close behind.

Into the trailer they both went. Grandma Sugar came along to be sure Cielo stayed quiet. He did. Off to the vet clinic we sped. I don't remember talking that much on the way.

When we got Cielo into the examination stocks at the clinic, our veterinarian kept calling out for anyone within earshot to "Come on over, you can stick your arm in here up to the elbow and touch this colt's carotid artery!"

Well, I can't say I shared his enthusiasm about reaching so deeply into Cielo's chest.

Thanks to the skills of Dr. Justin High, who became our primary veterinarian, Cielo was packed, laced up, and healed perfectly. When we sold him to the airline pilot and his family later that year there was barely a scar. That he had no major injury was amazing; the fact that there was no scar seemed to me almost a miracle in and of itself.

It is important to tell you that the smooth-wire horse fence supported with cedar stays every twelve inches—while only a year old—got pulled out and replaced with pipe and V-mesh. I never allowed wire of any kind in a cross-fence again. It was a long stretch of fence—probably fourteen hundred feet or so—but it got replaced pronto. Did I mention that horses aren't cheap?

The Horses Were Gone

As I drove up to the pilot's place it was obvious they didn't live there anymore. There was a brand new panel arena in the front pasture with two beautiful gray horses nurdling around in the burnt summer grass.

Okay, it would have been just too easy to drive up and ask if I could buy Cielo back. Where was the challenge in that? And, there would have been no message for me to share with you.

While driving home I realized the plan was no longer to simply fill Sky's empty place. This was now God's plan. Sky's boys *must* be found and brought home.

The new plan meant research. Where were the pilot and his family? Did they still have the Appaloosas? I dug through one of the junk drawers in our office to find a very old address and telephone book and called a lady who had been friends with the pilot's family. It had, after all, been nine years since we sold the horses.

All this happened on a Thursday. It was August, it was hot, and I was motivated; I had been commanded to find the horses. I *needed* to find them.

~ ~ ~

In prayer we worship the God of the Bible as our heavenly Father, as the Son who lived a human life, and as the Holy Spirit who dwells within us. Have you ever taken the time to really think through the concept of the Trinity?

The variety of relationships that are offered is, to my mind at least, the unfathomably miraculous part.

The concept of an omnipotent God is something we can all kind of work with. But what about a Savior who was completely divine and yet truly human, One who left real human footprints in the dusty roads of Jerusalem alongside both friends and enemies? This truth is so supernatural that it provides food for thought for which our appetite will never be satiated.

But the most amazing part to me is the Spirit that lives *within* us.

Our God is a personal God. He spoke an entire creation into existence solely for me, yet designed it just as purposefully for you.

When God looks down from His carnelian and jasper throne, His gaze goes individually to each child, recognized, prized, and loved as if each were His sole heir. As He was lifted upon the cross, Jesus had my name on His heart... He had your name on His lips. Our God is personal.

As the Holy Spirit prepares to enter into communion with each beloved child of the King, He doesn't select the one most worthy or the one most beautiful. He came looking for *me*. It was personal. He came looking for *you*. It was personal.

When Baber and I set out to bring home one of Sky's offspring, we went looking specifically for Ace, and Shiner. We were not shopping for a horse. We were not checking out what Appaloosas were on the market. We weren't even researching *which* of Sky's foals were for sale.

We went looking for these two by name, as individuals. No other horses could possibly fill the empty place in our pasture and in our hearts. We already had plenty of horses. We had no great excess of pasture. But we had a need to fill the empty place in our family. We needed to have Ace, Shiner, or (we hoped) Cielo.

We began the search.

God Still Works Miracles

Thankfully, the lady I called still had the same cell phone number. That, in and of itself, was pretty amazing to me. She picked up on my first try and told me that the pilot's family had moved over the past winter. The Appaloosas had been sold nearly a year before they'd moved.

The next part of the conversation was completely unexpected. The lady asked, "Did you see the picture of your horses in the newspaper?" I had no idea what she was talking about...

It seems there had been an article on the front page of a section of the *Fort Worth Star Telegram* the week before, focusing on the sad state of the horse economy and how little many horses were valued and thus headed for slaughter. We don't get the Fort Worth paper.

Ready for this? The pictures that accompanied the article were of two of Sky's boys, Cielo's brothers, Ace and Shiner. Sometimes God isn't just a still, small voice, but a very visible director of circumstances.

Armed with this information and a phone number for the pilot's wife, I thanked the lady and placed another call. No answer. I left a message and turned to my trusty computer.

While I may be technologically stunted, I do know how to research. I found the article in the *Star Telegram*. I found a reference to the place where my Appaloosa boys were. I saw pictures of Ace and Shiner. Even in the newspaper photograph reproduced on my laptop screen, I could see a part of Sky in each of them.

It had been nine years since I last saw Shiner and Ace. When we sold them they were just babies. Now they were completely mature horses, indeed older than any horse we owned except old Sally, a thirty-year-old retired broodmare. Yet, I recognized them immediately.

After hours of keystrokes and dead-ends, I finally found a telephone listing and address for what I hoped was the ranch where the boys were. It was Friday night. I took a chance and called the number. No answer. I left a message. With nothing else to do for the moment, I closed the computer.

How amazing. How miraculous. Just as I recognized the need to find Sky's boys, I discovered they had been featured in the newspaper—and on a front page with pictures!

My Appaloosa boys were still in Texas!

Saturday morning I checked for messages. Nothing. I returned to the newspaper's site and looked at the pictures of Shiner and Ace again. I could easily have picked them out of a line-up, even though they were now nine years old. Sky always passed much of himself on to his foals.

When morning became afternoon without a call, I tried the pilot's wife again. Success! She told me they had sold Snip well before the geldings. She told me the boys had gone to a wonderful home, a riding academy. The three boys were sold as a package, tack and all. It was comforting to know they had gone together and to a good place.

It was a relief to have confirmation that my research had brought me to the right place, that the phone number I'd used to leave a message the night before was correct. I called the number again and left another message.

By bedtime that night, there was still no return call. Although the address I'd found on-line was more than an hour and a half from our home, Baber and I decided we could not wait. We planned to drive up to the address we had after church the next day. Since the place was a public riding business, we figured it should be open on Sunday, right?

Wrong.

As we made our way along the very long exit ramp off the Interstate, I noticed a large pasture off to the right: steep hills with deep, low spots between them, dry, sparse grass, and a number of thin horses scattered among the few trees. My first thought was, *Poor horses.*

After making a sharp right turn onto the road we were looking for, my next thought was, *Oh no, this can't be the place.* It was.

The gate at the road was closed and locked. While neatly kept, the small arena was empty, and there were no horses visible. They were all out on the dry hills we had seen as we exited from the highway. We drove all this way and there was no one here.

I tried calling the phone number again. Again, no answer. I left yet another message.

For a moment we considered squeezing through the gate and walking in, but decided against it. Gates that are closed and locked do not invite strangers. We were strangers.

Baber and I were almost ready to give up for the day and drive off when we noticed a white pick-up pull into the short drive next door. A man got out and headed toward the empty pens we could see past the far end of the arena. I don't remember whether we hollered to get his attention or if he saw us on his own. The important part is he came over to talk with us.

The owner was helping someone move that day, and this gentleman was lending his support to that enterprise as well. He wasn't even supposed to be at the riding place, but wanted to check on water for some critters behind the barn.

We asked if the Appaloosas from the article were still there. Yes, they were. We asked if all three were there. "Yes." We told the man that we had owned them all, as well as their parents. He was gracious enough to offer us entry and told us we could go out into the pasture to visit the horses. The gate was opened and we drove in.

So, what are the odds that just as we needed the gate opened, someone miraculously appeared to do just that?

Actually, when God is at work, calculating odds is easy. They are always 100 percent.

JUST IN TIME

When we most need to be found, God is always faithful to do so. It is comforting to know that He cares for horses even as He does each tiny sparrow.

The events of the past three days led us on a precise path to this moment. Baber and I walked through the gate to the dry, hilly pasture and started the long walk toward the closest horse. Not anticipating a hike on such uneven terrain, I was stupidly wearing shorts and flip-flops. It didn't matter. I would have headed out across that pasture barefoot if necessary.

There were a few places where we had to find the best way to get across washouts and pick through some rocky places, but we soon made it down the first long hill and up the next.

"And the Lord shall help them and deliver them;
He shall deliver them from the wicked,
And save them,
Because they trust in Him." -- Psalm 37:40

There was the odd horse here and there, but no groups standing together in the usual manner of most horse herds. The gentleman who let us in had told us there were

[39]

about twenty horses in the pasture. So far we had seen two. Neither of the two was familiar to us and we had yet to see one of our Appaloosas. We trekked on.

Shiner

After climbing to the top of another hill we saw an Appaloosa, a bay roan with a large white blanket. His mane and tail were almost non-existent. This poor horse was sunburned, thin, scratched, chewed up a bit, and still wearing dried sweat marks from the last time he was saddled—whenever that was. The folks here called him by some other name, but this was our Shiner. No question.

Shiner's mother, Scotch Lace, was my favorite mare of all time. Scotch was stunningly beautiful, royally bred, honest, bold, and would have offered her life for me. Shiner was sired by Abduls Bright Sky, a proven champion in conformation, pedigree, and performance. Shiner was born to be a prince in the show pen, or at the very least, a beloved companion to someone who would appreciate him.

The horse standing twenty feet in front of us appeared to be an example of some of the worst clichés about Appaloosas. After taking in the reality before me, I was not only heartbroken, but also confused. Some Appaloosas have very sparse tails, the genetics for what are commonly known as rat tails passed along in certain bloodlines. Shiner carried none of those bloodlines.

Both Sky and Scotch had thick tails. Every year I had to cut six to eight inches off Sky's tail just to keep him from stepping on it. I could figure out the sunburn, the leanness, the nicks and bites. I could understand the dirty sweat marks. I could not figure out the absence of mane and tail hair.

Shiner also had a very odd top line. The area where his back met his croup sported an odd lump. I had seen similar cases on horses with major back injuries. It was a big bump. We knew he had been ridden, both from the saddle marks and from the man who let us into the pasture.

Indeed, although the gentleman was quite large, and Shiner looked so tiny, he said he had ridden Shiner recently, though it had been something of a challenge. The story of Shiner's behavior with him might have sounded like disobedience to some, but what I heard was an example of pairing an inexperienced rider with a very insecure horse. It was not a pretty picture.

I walked up to Shiner and made a slow circle around him. He didn't move. He didn't even seem to notice me. He didn't seem to care; even when I walked up to pet his thin neck and lightly rub my hand over his cheek. There was no recognition when I called his name. "Shiner."

It was time to move on. Where were Ace and Cielo?

Ace

As we turned away from Shiner and walked deeper into the parched, rolling hills of the pasture, we saw a chestnut gelding standing above us on the side of yet another hill. We had a full-profile view of him. Baber asked if that might be Ace. Ace has no Appaloosa coloring, so is pretty plain with just a white star on his dark face.

This horse was similarly marked, but I knew it couldn't be Ace. It may have been nearly a decade since I had seen him last, but I told my husband there was no way that Sky and Julie's DNA could have been mixed to produce a horse that was built like this one. Nope, couldn't happen.

You already know who Sky is; Julie Freckles Q is Ace's dam. Like Sky, Julie is another great example of what is best about Appaloosas. Julie is black with a light sprinkling of white on her rump and was a Reserve National Champion reining horse. Julie is also Cielo's mother, Cielo being just a year older than his full-brother, Ace. Julie was beautiful, well put together, and there was no way this gelding was by Sky and out of Julie. As far as I know, Julie is still producing reining prospects for her current owners, although she must be getting up there in age by now.

Several hills bottomed out to create a low place further into the pasture. There was a small stand of trees that hid what I assumed (hoped) was a watering hole. We headed in that direction, calling out for Ace and Cielo as we picked our way through tall, black weed stalks that seemed to be the only plant remnants in the hot, dry dirt of this pasture.

As we topped the next rise, we saw a solid-colored chestnut horse slowly make his way up the hill from the opposite side. Without a doubt, this was Ace. It was easy to recognize his head even from a distance. Sky always stamped his foals. I had seen part of Sky in Shiner, and I saw a bit of Sky walking up the hill toward us now.

Ace stopped well short of our position. Baber and I moved quietly toward him. He wasn't as lethargic as Shiner. Ace actually noticed we were there. Not wanting to make any sudden move that would send Ace back deeper into the pasture, I pretended not to see him. I wandered in the general direction of his side, being careful not to look directly at him. Horses often get nervous and will retreat when a strange human marches directly up to them. Horses often interpret such moves as a threat. Eventually I made my way to him and reached out to lightly scratch his withers.

After nine years Ace and I met again. Like Shiner, he too was thin, his coat dull, nicked up, and scruffy looking. Ace had worn out the bottom of his mane, and although his tail was still thick and long, nearly all the hair along the top of his tailbone was rubbed down to bristles or skin. There were open sores on his tail and on his rump both above and beside the tail head itself. He looked just like horses that have had their tails "done" too many times by too many bad veterinarians. His rump was a mass of scars, sores and lumps.

After Shiner, Ace's appearance wasn't the shock it might have been otherwise. Baber and I took turns quietly stroking Ace, inspecting him from head to hoof.

When you're Family, Pretty Doesn't Matter

Weren't Shiner and Ace just the worst examples of Sky's progeny? It certainly seemed so. They sure didn't look like the beautiful, highborn horses they were supposed to be. Neither would have gotten a second look at a sale, and doubtful any buyer would make a bid, should they be offered.

I was reminded of the story of Black Beauty, a well-bred horse of great character and elegance until circumstance and poor care reduced him to life as a dull, damaged, joyless creature. Black Beauty nearly met his end at a low-end horse sale. No serious bidder would want to take him home and care for him. The only probable outcome, outside of a miracle, would be a final walk to the knackers (slaughterhouse) and a brutal end.

Beauty's friend from better days, a chestnut mare named Ginger, when fallen into equally hard times, told him, "I wish I was dead. I have seen dead horses, and I am sure

[43]

they do not suffer pain. I wish I may drop down dead at my work and not be sent off to the knackers."

Readers are simply heartbroken when they turn the page and find Black Beauty at the auction, waiting for his sentence. We want to leap directly into the pages of the book to buy him or shout to everyone that "This is Black Beauty! Don't you know him?"

The miracle is yet to come. Readers must patiently read on. Black Beauty will eventually be recognized by the only one who matters. Readers just need to wait for events to play out before judging the story.

Seldom do the human characters come out looking good in animal stories. Most of the sadness visited on animals is delivered by human hands. My mother always stayed as far away as possible from books, movies, or television shows about animals for this very reason.

But, Black Beauty found his miracle and happy ending, and now that we had found Ace and Shiner, they would also have one.

God is not a respecter of persons. Like the simple and honest horses who cross our path, God doesn't care how wealthy we are, what our earthly pedigree is, what our social status is, or how beautiful we are of form or face. In the family of Jesus Christ, beauty has nothing to do with what is visible to the human eye.

"For the Lord your God is God of gods… mighty and awesome, who shows no partiality and accepts no bribes." -- Deuteronomy 10:17

"For with the Lord our God there is no injustice or partiality or bribery." -- 2 Chronicles 19:7

The beauty of Ace and Shiner to us is in our family connection. And that is a good thing, because the horses we found in the dry place that day certainly wouldn't get anyone's vote for pretty. Likewise, what a blessing that God looks far beyond what others see when He loves us as His own—rubs, scars, saddle marks and all.

There was still the question of Cielo. Where was he? In what condition would we find beautiful Cielo? We continued to search the pasture until it became evident that he just wasn't there. We had counted out the full number of horses who were supposed to be in the pasture. The man said Cielo was one of them… he was mistaken.

The nice gentleman who had let us into the pasture drove his truck all the way around and picked us up from the far side. We told him we were interested in buying both Ace and Shiner. The lady that owned them had gotten our phone messages and had told him she had already decided to sell them. Neither Ace nor Shiner was working out for her, and she needed them off the feed bill.

It turned out that Cielo had been sold nine months earlier. He had been welcomed into a home and family where he was loved and was being shown by a twelve-year-old girl. We left a message with the agent who had handled the sale that if at any time the family wanted to sell Cielo, we would be interested in buying him back. There were no plans to sell him anytime soon. We'll wait.

Cielo is beautiful. Cielo has a winning personality and is well broke. We had wanted him back with us for just those same reasons. He was pretty, talented, well-adjusted, and would be a member of our family who would draw oohs and ahhs from everyone who saw us with him. We could be proud of him.

[45]

We had gone looking for all three of Sky's boys. Cielo had a home; Shiner and Ace needed a home. Shiner and Ace were the last of Sky's offspring, foaled the same year we gelded Sky. They were both the first and last Appaloosas born into our family after we moved from Arizona to Texas.

There was no decision to be made. We had gone looking for them. We had found them. They were going to come home.

Another Lesson Learned

By the time we pulled into the garage after our long day of driving and traipsing across the barren pasture in Roanoke, we were more exhausted from emotion than the exertion of climbing hills under the hot Texas sun.

During the drive home my husband and I talked about Sky and his boys, Ace and Shiner. We would get them home, no matter what it took. Both of us recognized the handiwork of the Lord in the events of the past few days that would forever change our lives.

Isn't it just like humans to want what is beautiful, to desire partners who make us look good by simply standing next to them? We are naturally drawn to what is prettiest, what is newest, choosing what we think is the best. That's exactly why Cielo had been our first choice. Cielo was prettier, Cielo was broke; he didn't need remedial work. Cielo would make us look good. God, in His perfect wisdom, knew better.

The path to Shiner and Ace couldn't have been more obvious had it been paved with gold and lit with neon signs. Ever since I first realized that God used my horses to help me better understand my relationship with Him, the lessons have been stacking up. *Amazing Grays, Amazing Grace* was the product of a first whole series of lessons. *He Came*

[47]

Looking for Me is a curriculum of continuing education for me.

The lesson I learned that day is that beauty is in spirit and not a product of physical appearance. Families are knit together from much more than resemblance of face or form, but by unity of spirit and relationship. I began the day looking for the pretty one and ended the day determined to bring home the damaged ones instead.

Love is a word that describes relationship. Love has nothing to do with physical beauty. Finding Cielo and bringing him home would have prevented the opportunity for me to learn this lesson it appeared I still needed to master. While it would have been easy to proudly ride Cielo out before any audience, I now understand that I will be more blessed to victoriously ride the horse who may be the least beautiful Sky ever produced.

Even on that first day, I realized that Shiner's beauty to me comes from the relationships I cherished with his parents, Scotch and Sky. Shiner is a gift from God, allowing me another chance to deserve the answer to prayer that Sky had been—an answer I missed by at least half a mile.

There are no coincidences. It was one year ago today, last Good Friday, that I wrote what would become the final chapter of *Amazing Grays, Amazing Grace*. The title of that chapter is "The Spotted Wonder," the story of my relationship with Sky and how I blew the opportunity I had been given.

Just today this question appeared in my email in-box: "Why didn't God answer my prayer and keep my horse from dying?" I wouldn't have known how to answer that question until recently.

God sent me Sky in answer to my prayer for a horse to share my life with. He was the perfect answer. I didn't accept God's wonderful gift with the humility it deserved. Sky was truly an amazing horse and I succumbed to the temptation to capitalize on this gift from God to seek success as a trainer and breeder. I did not recognize the true beauty of what God had literally dropped into my lap the moment Sky was born.

When God closes a door it remains closed forever, but He is also faithful to provide a new opening, be it window or door. The door to repairing my mistakes with Sky was closed and sealed when he died. Shiner and Ace are new windows that promise fresh opportunities. Now I understand and will not fail them as I did Sky.

Sometimes we lose a precious relationship, whether horse or human, when there is another lesson God wants us to learn. New lessons come with new relationships. For whatever reason, we seem to create habits that we either don't realize we picked up or simply can't overcome. God sometimes ends one relationship and replaces it with another that will better serve us in the long run.

Another big lesson came as a result of the conviction born in my husband and me to find Ace and Shiner. That experience led to our appreciation of the scriptural promise that among those whom God has chosen, none will be lost. We did not set out to find just any horse, much less any Appaloosa, or even any foal of Sky's. There are lots of them. We set out to find these specific individuals—no substitutions.

Jesus knows each of us by name. There is no substituting any one for any other. For those of us not home

[49]

yet, He has made provision. None will be forgotten, lost, or replaced. Not one.

COMING HOME

The first thing the next morning, the phone rang. It was the lady who owned Ace and Shiner. She was interested in selling them. They were not working out for her and she had already decided to move them out. Both Ace and Shiner had each come with a little more baggage that she was either not prepared to, or didn't want to, handle. We settled on a reasonable price for the two and I told her we would be there by noon. Don't tell anyone, but I would have paid whatever it cost to get my boys home.

Our trailer was hooked up without delay; halters and lead ropes were tossed quickly into the tack room. Small flakes of alfalfa hay went into two of the mangers and fresh shavings were placed onto the floor mats. Not knowing how well Ace and Shiner loaded into a trailer, I went prepared for all contingencies.

Baber and I set out on the road that Labor Day morning as excited as two little kids on Christmas Eve. We arrived at the lady's place about eleven o'clock—just two hours after speaking with her for the very first time. Ace and Shiner were up in pens having a bite to eat. The lady was busy with a few other people, and horses were being tacked up and groomed. It looked like a regular day at any riding stable.

After greeting Shiner and Ace, we spent a little time talking with the lady. I really liked her, and I have no doubt she genuinely cares for the horses. The only thing I have never been able to resolve is why they were in such poor condition. God works in mysterious ways, and this was, after all, His plan.

We learned that Shiner would be easy to load; Ace, not so much. We were told that Ace had issues being under roofs or covers. He had the most idiosyncrasies it seems, and I figured I might as well start our relationship off on the proper foot. I prepared to teach Ace to load into a trailer.

Loading a horse in a trailer, to me, is actually trailer training. I don't want to just get the horse loaded; I want to build foundation for the next time the horse needs to load and the time after that, and so on.

Let's just say that it took a bit of doing, but Ace learned to trust me enough to walk into the trailer—six times. I always like to start with six times. Shiner loaded up behind Ace, and we settled accounts.

Our faces beamed brighter than any star as we set out from what *had* been, on the way to what *would* be. As we drove Ace and Shiner home from Roanoke, Baber and I reminisced about Sky, Scotch, and Julie. We marveled at the whirlwind we'd been riding the past several days.

Ace and Shiner were actually in the trailer behind us. The last time they were in a trailer behind us, they were still being carried by their mothers when we moved from Arizona to Texas. Today they were coming home. You would have thought we had snared amazing deals on two of the most valuable horses in the world. And in one sense, we had.

One of the greatest gifts possible in life is watching the hand of God at work. So often He works in secret, or at least works in ways we are too blind to see. Since our experience with *Amazing Grays,* we have been blessed on a regular basis with ringside seats in His theater. Today was simply another act in the play.

The hand of God brought Ace and Shiner home to us. The meaning was clear to us as our Dodge truck ate up the miles on the road back home. Ace and Shiner were given to us as a clear example of the faithfulness of Jesus Christ. There would be another message for us to share.

Once Baber backed the trailer up to the barn, we unloaded Ace and Shiner. Part of teaching Ace to load into the trailer included teaching him to back out. So far, he remembered his lessons. Shiner and Ace were soon out of the trailer. Baber had Shiner; I had Ace. They were now free to take a look at their new home.

They only had eyes for each other.

We had to encourage Ace a bit to get him to walk into the barn and down the breezeway to the arena gate. There was bright-green, juicy grass growing around the edges where the fence separated the arena from the pasture that would give both Ace and Shiner something to nibble on while we readied their pen.

The idea that we would be adding two souls to the family was so new that we had yet to prepare a separate paddock in one pasture. Since the boys had not had green grass in some time, we wanted to be certain they were introduced to our rich pasture a bit at a time to prevent colic or founder.

As Ace and Shiner stood in the arena, we started hauling Priefert fence panels to construct a large pen off the small barn. Ace and Shiner would have shade, water, and feed in the pen while they were gradually weaned on to pasture over the next week.

Fresh water filled a half-barrel; an eight-foot feed bunk was filled with coastal Bermuda hay and two scoops of high-protein, high-fat pellets. A second pile of good hay was placed under the shade next to the water barrel. We had been told that Ace wouldn't go under a cover, so we made sure he could reach the water without having to stand under the cover.

Once all was prepared, we returned to the arena to pick up the boys and lead them to their new home. Before we opened the gate, we took pictures of them to keep as a reminder.

Shiner and Ace walked quietly with us to their new home. Once in through the small gate, they were ready to begin life again. After a final pet, the halters came off and we retreated to our front porch to watch the boys settle in.

It was sunny and hot. Shiner and Ace walked slowly around the pen. We had only paneled an area about sixty feet square, so it wasn't a very long trip.

Shiner found the pellets. Ace soon joined him at the feeder. As the afternoon progressed, Shiner appeared to be the leader, just the opposite of what we had been told by the lady in Roanoke.

By dinnertime, the boys were content to chew on a little hay, and both had found the water barrel. Funny, but Ace had no problem going under the shade to examine the hay and take a long drink. Ace and Shiner were doing well,

[54]

but didn't seem to have much of an appetite. Once the pellets were gone, they mostly just stood about, keeping each other company.

Freedom

Sometimes we don't recognize freedom even when we have it.

The next morning, we fed the boys more pellets and left them to work on the hay that remained. As thin as they were, it was a bit surprising that Shiner and Ace didn't just snarf up everything in the feeder. Yet they didn't. The pellets went over well, but eating didn't seem to be a real priority for either of them.

We were a little concerned about turning Shiner and Ace out into the bright-green pasture full of rich grass. Would they overeat? Would they want to go back to the pen? What would happen when they got out and could visit with the very curious horses on the opposite sides of three cross-fences?

As is usually the case, our worries were unfounded, but not in a good way. We opened the panel gate and pushed the boys out into the pasture. We closed the gate behind them so they wouldn't just head back to the place they knew was safe and well-stocked with food and water.

Our horses shared fence lines with Ace and Shiner on the east and west. The south fence was shared with a neighbor whose three horses were very interested in the new kids in town. Horses were hollerin' and running the fence lines on every side, trying to get Ace and Shiner to come over and chat.

When the gate opened, Baber and I watched Ace and Shiner s-l-o-w-l-y walk out into the pasture, side by side as if hitched together by an invisible harness. They didn't stop to graze. Neither of them looked to the right or to the left as they trudged along like slow-motion robots. I had never seen such a thing before. Ace and Shiner were not exhibiting behavior that in any way resembled that of normal horses.

Ace and Shiner were damaged spirits. They didn't appear to even notice the excited horses competing for their attention. What should have been tempting, lush grass didn't get as much as a sniff from either of them. Their heads remained low, eyes forward, as they slowly walked out into the pasture like zombies.

Sometime later, Ace and Shiner realized there was grass beneath their hooves. A nibble here, a taste there—we sure didn't have to worry about them overdoing the grass thing. What we did have to consider was how to get enough calories into the boys to get their appetites started up again. You can lead a horse to water, but you can't make him drink. You can put food in the feeder, but you can't make a horse eat.

Instead of restricting Ace and Shiner's time in the pasture to only two hours as we had originally planned, we left them out for six. At suppertime, we opened the gate to the pen, put pellets in the feeder, and let the boys in. They came back immediately and seemed to feel safer in the smaller pen than the larger pasture.

We did not add any more hay. I have found that sometimes horses will eat more when you let them run out of food than if you keep adding more to an untouched pile. Feeding smaller amounts more frequently gets more calories into picky ones than sticking with the usual, twice-a-day feeding schedule. It's better to let a horse look for just a bit more than to have one walk away from a feeder holding unwanted rations.

Horses crave routine. When scheduling or inconsistent owners prevent horses from enjoying a daily routine, many horses learn to consider non-routine to actually be their normal routine. For Ace and Shiner, we wanted to create security by providing a set routine from the very first day.

The next few weeks were simple. Ace and Shiner gradually learned that they were always safe, always fed, that Baber and I showed up regular as clockwork each day—and we sometimes arrived with horse cookies in hand.

We began to add basic grooming to their schedule. Their poor coats were so dry, and each of them was missing a significant amount of hair. After a soothing bath, we began regular sessions with a soft-rubber curry. The relaxing skin massage was good for the boys; the attention from us with no strings attached was even more therapeutic than the simple grooming they enjoyed.

I was still confused by Shiner's lack of tail hair, but he gradually started filling in the hairless areas on his face, shoulders, and rump. Without any tail hair, he had a tough time fighting flies and keeping the hot sun off his little white cheeks (not on his face...). The skin between his cheeks would normally be protected by tail hair. Without that natural barrier to the blazing Texas rays, the pink skin of his behind was constantly raw and peeling from sunburn.

Daily applications of salve with sunscreen were added after the grooming session ended. Shiner began to look forward to the relief the cream brought and soon learned to stand quietly while I doctored his hind end.

[57]

As time passed, Ace and Shiner began to spend more time grazing. The odd lump on Shiner's back gradually disappeared as he put on weight. Ace's coat began to shine.

Ace also began rubbing his tail. Hard. On anything he could find. Then he started rubbing the base of his mane. Now I knew how he got all the scars and wounds on his rump. I had known it was from rubbing, but didn't know exactly what caused it. The first month or so he was home, he had not rubbed at all. Now he was making up for lost time.

Family Secrets

Since I knew Ace's mother well, I had a pretty good idea of what caused such extreme discomfort that he would tear bark off the lone tree in the pasture trying to calm his itch. When the thick layer of bark ripped off the tree, it usually took hair and hide with it.

Scratching always begins with an original irritation that, left unresolved, can become a nasty, nasty habit. It seems Ace had a long history of scratching. Whatever part habit played in his scratching, it was well entrenched.

When dealing with bad habits, the trick is to eliminate what caused the habit in the first place and then address the habit itself before it becomes nearly impossible to break. This is pretty much true with horses and humans.

Everyone knows the extreme behavior addictions can cause. Some bad habits begin from pure happenstance. Others are created when we copy the actions of another— again, true for both humans and horses. Finally, a bad habit or vice may be created when an individual is either under extreme pressure or pain of some kind and discovers a way to mask or hide from that pain.

[58]

At some point in his life, Ace found a way to calm his itch by scratching. I don't know yet whether he is scratching here because there is something now creating an itch or if he has settled in well enough to finally remember that he has a habit of scratching.

Julie, Ace's mother, began scratching like the dickens the second year she was in Texas. We never had any problems while she was in Arizona, but that last year we had her, she rubbed her neck and sides until there were raw spots on her previously perfect, black coat.

At first I thought that insects were bugging her in the pasture. We tried different fly sprays and a scrim sheet, but the problem continued. Finally I brought her into the barn to get serious about fixing the problem. Not only was I concerned for Julie's comfort, but we had decided to only breed Quarter Horses and had to sell our remaining Appaloosa mares. Julie needed to look the part of the champion she was in order to make the best sale possible.

There are probably a dozen remedies to soothe skin and coat irritation in horses. I tried them all. None of them worked. Finally I called our regular vet out to see if he had any better ideas. He didn't.

About this time, the vet we had been using left the group practice to go out on his own. The emergency with Cielo introduced us to another vet at the clinic, Dr. High. While working with him one day, I mentioned Julie's problem. He asked if we had tested her for allergies. "Nope," I replied, "we haven't tried that yet."

After spending two hundred fifty dollars for the allergy test, we finally had an answer to our dilemma. Julie was allergic to just about everything that grew in the pastures

HE CAME LOOKING FOR ME

of Texas, as well as a lot of the bagged feed sold locally. Bermuda, rye, oats—all of the grasses and feed we had in abundance caused Julie's scratching issue. She was not allergic to alfalfa. We bought alfalfa for the first time since we'd gotten to Texas.

Once I switched Julie to a diet consisting of nothing but alfalfa hay, she quickly quit scratching and her coat returned to normal—soft, glossy, and blue-black as a raven's wing. We sold her to folks from out of state who had the allergy test results to fall back on should they ever have a similar problem with her. As far as I know, all has been well.

Ace is probably allergic to the feed Texas horses normally receive, including the grass of improved pastures. The process of finding a solution has begun. We'll see what we need to do to keep him comfortable. I know what worked for Julie. We are committed to Ace and will do whatever is necessary.

Sometimes you have to take a lot of remedial steps before you can actually work your way up to taking that first step forward. As far as Shiner and Ace are concerned, we were just about there.

COME UNTO ME

"The secret of life is relationship with God. The important question is not how, why, where, or when; the important question is 'Who?'" -- Amazing Grays, Amazing Grace

The secret of life has not changed since I wrote *Amazing Grays*, nor has the content of the important question we all must ask ourselves if we pursue a relationship with God. God is not about what; He is all about Who.

Not long after the Appaloosa boys came home I went out to feed one morning to find Ace and Shiner walking along the fence that separated their pasture from our backyard. I take care of the horses in the main barn and Baber takes care of the front barn and pastures. He would feed Ace and Shiner, but here they were.

I tried to spend part of every day with each horse, giving them all individual attention, working on each unique relationship. As I considered what I might do with Ace and Shiner that day, it occurred to me that I could begin their day with a couple of carrots.

Baber was just getting ready to go out to the little barn, and I knew I would be hard pressed to get Ace and Shiner to ignore him and come to see me at the backyard fence. Why? Ace and Shiner would probably not come to me because they still associate food with a place and not with a person. They think that blessings are only found at the feeder, that the important question in life includes the where, when, and the how of routine.

"Come unto me." Matthew 11:28

I asked Baber to take his time getting on boots and rounding up cat food before leading the morning parade of hungry felines to the front barn. Preparing for my foray into the pasture, I detoured through the garage to swap out barn boots for backyard shoes. I grabbed a bag of carrots from the fridge and hurried out the door to the backyard fence.

Ace and Shiner had moved to be in position to meet Baber at their feeder, ready for the morning's provision. My first few calls to them went without any movement in my direction. They turned to look at me; they knew I was there. But they still associated blessing (food) with a place and not with a person. They only thought about the "what" and not the "who." This is an area where there is foundation yet to be laid in our relationship.

I did not give up. There can frequently be a fine line between issuing an invitation and begging. I never beg a horse to do anything. Whenever I make an offer, there is always a limit attached. If it is not accepted within the established limits, the offer is withdrawn and I make a training note to address the cause for the refusal.

There is a radical difference between making an offer and issuing a request. An offer allows for a negative response; a request does not. This morning I made an offer of carrots in return for Ace and Shiner's presence and attention. Had I made a request, I would have been committed to taking whatever action was necessary to ensure that my request was complied with.

Christians often misunderstand the details of communication with God. Do you expect blessings to be attached to a place—your church, for instance? Do you expect to be blessed by following a prescribed routine? Do you attach more importance to the Bible than to its Author?

Do you concentrate on any question other than the "who" of life? If you do, may I suggest you reconsider? There is no security in the church building except, perhaps, from the elements. There is no security in the physical pages and words of the Bible, and no routine will guarantee you eternal life.

The only thing that matters is the God who leads your church, the God who breathed the words of the Bible, the God who created seasons, tides, and natural routine. All that matters is your personal relationship with God the Father, Jesus Christ our Savior, and the Holy Spirit, our teacher. All are one. God is the only correct answer to this most important question of "Who?" None other.

Shiner and Ace don't enjoy eternal security yet. Evidence of this is their attachment to place, to the feeder, and to routine. Once we establish a right relationship they will begin to look first to me, ignoring the where, what, and how of blessing. Ace and Shiner will find true security when all they consider is the "who"—seeing only me.

Let's go back to the carrot question of the morning. I gambled on the hope that I had already laid enough foundation with Ace and Shiner to stay at the fence and nudge my offer forward to where it might be considered a request. Having made this specific decision, I immediately began listing my options should the boys ignore my request.

We've been blessed with winter moisture for the first time in years, so the ground is muddy and spongy where there isn't standing water. I only had backyard shoes on, not trudge-through-the-mud boots. If the boys persisted in remaining in the *where* of blessing, I would need to get into the pasture and create movement in their feet. The broadest outline of action began to build as I called again. "Shiner, Ace."

Thankfully, feet began to move. Ace started to walk- not to me, but he began to walk. Shiner stood still, watching me. I called again. Ace turned and lined out in a direct path to where I stood at the fence. Once Shiner realized that Ace was committed to moving, he also started walking toward me.

That was a relief. I was prepared to slog on out into the pasture and make sure I got the boys' attention, but Ace saved my bacon. In the beginning, it seems Ace is the one most likely to accept my offer of relationship.

They both liked the carrots. The rest will be an adventure - and looks can be deceiving.

IT IS PERSONAL

One of the most important messages of *He Came Looking for Me* is that your relationship with Jesus Christ is a personal one.

When we went looking for horses in September 2009, we weren't looking for just any horses. We went looking for Appaloosas. But not just any Appaloosas; we wanted to find Sky's foals and bring them home. Our search was not for just any available progeny of his, but specifically for Adios Cielo, Clearly Cielo, and Signed by Sky.

Our purpose was to find these particular sons of Julie Freckles Q and Scotch Lace. We found them. Was it my great detective work that brought us together on the parched summer hills of Roanoke, Texas, or a supernatural act of God? My money is on God.

When Jesus Christ was born in the little stable in Bethlehem two millennia ago, He came to be a personal Savior. Jesus came to save sinful man. But not just any men, He came looking for the children of His Father so He could make arrangements that would bring each of them home. His search, His sacrifice, was not just for any available humans, but specifically for you; specifically for me.

As our search began for our Appaloosa boys, we did the equivalent of preparing engraved nameplates for their stall doors in our barn, placing those stalls on reserve. The

[65]

stalls would remain empty until the intended occupants were found, transported, and safely moved into their new home.

"In My Father's house are many mansions... I go to prepare a place for you." --John 14:2

Jesus has prepared a home for His redeemed in heaven. On each doorpost is an engraved nameplate with one name. There are a finite number of celestial mansions that sit empty, awaiting the homecoming of those for whom they are reserved.

The time is at hand. The Good Shepherd is busy rounding up His flock. He is searching among crowded cities, rural homesteads and wilderness expanses to find the specific individuals He seeks. Jesus has a list. The list was given Him by His Father. He will lose none that are on it.

That same list was at the foot of the cross, each name miraculously appearing, one by one, as the lifeblood of Jesus pooled in the sand at the foot of Calvary's tree. When the final name on the roll appeared, Jesus said, "It is finished."

There is no spiritual round-up intended to secure a particular number of souls for transport to heaven. There will be a limited number, but each in that number has a unique name and spirit. No substitutions will be allowed. If we were to make that journey by bus, each and every seat would have a name on it, and no other would be allowed to sit in someone else's seat.

Can you imagine how Black Beauty felt as he stood, head hanging ever so low, knees aching, waiting at the horse sale to meet his end? His spirit was broken; he didn't care to continue on. Life had beaten him down.

Did Black Beauty's life really hang in the balance? As Ace and Shiner's owner tried to decide how to move them out, were their futures truly in jeopardy?

Have you ever been in a place where you simply didn't care anymore? A place where life has beaten you down and your spirit feels broken? Most of us have, at one time or another. I know I have. One time I hit the skids and didn't slide—just stopped hard on the most unforgiving concrete slab of life on the last subfloor at the very, very bottom.

Each of us experiences the routine ups and downs with their varying degrees of difficulties every week, every month, and every year we live. What I'm talking about here is the absolute bottom where there is not one further inch to fall. You either lie there and die or else you go back up—there simply is no other option. There is no further down possible.

There But for the Grace of God

When you return from the lowest place possible, you achieve freedom from many fears that people who never hit bottom still harbor in the darkness of the night.

Here's one of the things I learned: there is no such thing on earth as a bottomless pit. There is a bottom. I know because I've been there. There's no beast down there in the unknown. Many times the monster you fear the most is the one staring back at you in the bathroom mirror every morning.

Another thing I learned is that a chosen child of God is never alone. We may choose to separate ourselves from Him, but He is always available if we decide to return. In those very dark places where we have no ability to get back to Him on our own, those times where our tiny reservoir of try is completely depleted, He will offer you a hand up. If you experienced the way back like I did, you won't actually see the work of His hand until a much later time when the light has returned and your vision with it.

Shiner and Ace had no option in choosing where they went. As is usually the case, decisions made that result in an animal or child being abandoned or abused are always made by men and women. Just the fact that you are reading this is proof that God reaches His hand out to us in many ways and in a variety of places.

Ace and Shiner could not choose to come home. Their fate depended upon the people who cared, or did not care, for them. But, God had a plan. They would not be forgotten. They were found and brought home just as you will be.

Why were they chosen? They were chosen for you. If we had not been sent to bring home Ace and Shiner, there would be no book. If there were no book, you would not have this opportunity to believe that you will be redeemed—just when you are most in need.

No matter how dire your circumstances today, even if you are sored up, burnt out, and believe yourselves to be abandoned in a vast wasteland, the Redeemer is working in the background, and you too, dear brother or sister in Christ, will come home.

A few days ago, I got an update from a father whose son had been out in the world alone, addicted, and apart from his family the last time the dad and I spoke. The father had lived for months not knowing whether his son still lived or had died in some filthy alley.

Since the last time we talked, the story had radically changed. From the depths of hell on earth, the son had returned. Not only had he returned, but he was claiming higher ground every day in sober service to his Lord and his fellows. Now a student and minister, the son is a charismatic speaker to others who also crushed their noses while lying face down on the bottom.

The father is now filled with joy, awe, and hope as he watches his son begin this new journey. The important concept to remember is that while we may not know where a loved one is—we know where God is. There is none so lost that God doesn't know exactly where they are at every single moment.

In the prisons, shelters, and graveyards of this country, there are folks who walked some of the same paths I did. Why the difference? The simple answer is the grace of God. Only by grace was I kept from going so far down the road that I couldn't find my way back.

Are the people in the prisons and shelters today lost forever? I don't know and neither does anyone else. If their name is in the Book of Life, they will not be lost. I have a mansion reserved for me. Shiner had a stall reserved for him. He's already home and I'm looking forward to reaching mine one day.

Spending time in the valleys of life is similar to time spent on the mountain tops. It is impossible to live exclusively on the heights of experience and equally impossible to suffer forever at the bottom. During the times when we are face down at the bottom, nose smashed in the dirt, we think we are alone and lost. Shiner and Ace believed they were alone and lost. They were not, I was not, and neither are you.

[69]

Do you think life is a Lottery?

If you are sitting under the darkest cloud you can imagine wondering how your life will end, do you really believe there's some sort of Life Lottery? Do you think that wining depends on some roll of the cosmic dice? Do you feel like your luck has run out?

Do you know Jesus Christ? If you do, then you know that the book of your days has already been written, and the final chapter is printed in indelible ink. Like *Black Beauty*, one simply needs to work through the remaining pages to arrive at the blessed conclusion.

Knowing how your story ends and whether the remaining chapters contain joy or heartache depends upon your relationship with Jesus Christ. Ace and Shiner had no idea that we were looking for them. The parched hillsides of Roanoke certainly promised no miracles. But, because of their relationship to Sky, Scotch, Julie, and us—the story of their lives was about to change.

Like Black Beauty, Ace and Shiner were broken spirits, enduring each successive day until their number finally counted down to the end. But, even though they felt completely alone we were busy looking for them. My friend's addicted son may have believed he was lost forever, but God was in the background working the entire time.

Everyone feels lost and abandoned at one time or another, but we are never alone. There is no such thing as a bottomless pit for children of the King. That's a lie meant to scare us into uncertainty. And you know where that lie comes from... You may not see what's being done on your behalf just at this moment, but as a chosen child of God, one

[70]

day you will walk in glory into your own mansion. That's no lottery, just a guaranteed fact.

The relationship we have with Jesus Christ is a personal one.

"...the sheep hear his voice; and calls his own sheep by name and leads them out. And when he brings out his own sheep, he goes before them; and the sheep follow him, for they know his voice." -- John 10:3

HE CAME LOOKING FOR ME

REFLECTION

We know that relationships are never static; they are always changing, either progressing or regressing. The frantic level of activity in the lives of many people today has all but eliminated a key element of proper worship as well as stunted the development of healthy relationships. What they are missing is time in their schedule for reflection.

Functioning relationships operate under one of two formulas, either from a habit of task or habit of obedience. The habit of task is what causes people or horses to act in a predictable manner based upon the circumstances surrounding them. Barrel horses are trained to run a pattern, and many will run just as true as they can regardless of who is in the saddle. Race horses that have lost their jockey still run as fast as they can to the finish line.

Unlike horses who are trained to a pattern, horses who respond from a habit of obedience are completely tuned in to their rider. They have a great deal of foundation and put all those pieces together in just the way the rider asks, no matter the circumstances. The difference between responding from a habit of task or from relationship is one of focus. Does your horse focus on the task at hand or on his relationship with you?

If you haven't thought about it recently, what is the quality of your other relationships? Are your kids obedient at

[73]

church but not at the mall? If so, then they are trained to the task and not to be obedient to their parents.

This question of task versus obedience came up this morning when I went to the barn to let the horses out to graze for the day. The continuing wet conditions have made it impossible for us to ride more than once or twice in the past couple of months, but I have good relationships with the horses and am well established as their leader. At least I thought so. Yes, we have well functioning relationships. But as we already know, relationships are always changing, getting better or getting worse. This morning I realized my horses have devolved from their usual habit of obedience to a habit of task. How did I know? What was the difference in their behavior? The horses weren't disrespectful, but they were not actively respectful either.

The most important element to amazing relationships is time spent together. When I don't spend regular time with my horses, the balance in our relationship account dwindles. The same is true of any relationship.

Our pastures do not have any stock tanks or the water holes of varying sizes that folks from outside Texas often call ponds. As I look across our sea of grass, I should not see bodies of water. For the last few months, however, we have been the land of ten thousand lakes due to the unusual and persistent rains in north central Texas.

Not that I'm complaining, mind you. We haven't had adequate subsoil moisture coming out of winter for years. Even though my riding options have been severely curtailed, I eagerly anticipate an abundance of coastal Bermuda next spring that will feed our horses until winter. Until we downsized and moved to what used to be one of our remote hayfields, I always had an indoor arena. Since retiring from the equine profession I couldn't justify the expense of building what is now a pure luxury. So, our riding schedule depends on the weather conditions just like most other horse owners.

As I entered the first stall this morning to let Asti out to graze, I realized she was waiting for my *action* (habit of task) and not my *direction* (habit of obedience.) Her eyes were on the gate, waiting for me to open it. I was just the vehicle that would get her where she wanted to go. Any interest in me was strictly self-serving. I'm sure you've had the same experience, whether it came from a spouse, a child, or a pet.

"Hurry up and do what I want!" Wow, where's the warmth and beauty of relationship in that particular message? When that command is delivered by a child, a horse, a student, or a pet, it is a sure sign that your leadership and authority has reached a dangerously low level. So, like every other good parent, leader, or horse trainer would—I switched to lesson mode with Asti.

It was time for Asti to forget about the gate and the pasture beyond and concentrate on me. I asked Asti to soften and obey my body language by yielding her body. She moved away from me rather than properly yielding to me. After only a minute of review, I easily regained Asti's attention and she was properly focused again. Out to the pasture she went. I repeated this with the other three horses. As I went down the line, I had to work just a bit longer with each one in order to get Swizzle, Bo, and Copper into obedience mode and their minds off the grass.

Since I had not planned to be giving lessons this morning, I had neither halter nor lead rope with me when I opened the door to Asti's stall. The best way to make a point is to react immediately when we encounter less-than-perfect behavior. Improvising, I used my hand on the bridge of the each horse's nose as I asked them in turn to bend their head around toward me. Once each neck and jaw softened, I looked at the horse's hip and "suggested" he or she yield it softly. We got it done (after a fashion), and I left the barn with the knowledge that I was guilty of failing to maintain a proper relationship with each of our horses.

Many owners might have walked back to the house and wondered just what was wrong with their usually obedient horse. "Why was Asti so pushy? Maybe tomorrow she'll be back to her usual self." Well, maybe—but maybe not. The fault of failing to maintain the relationship properly was mine and the responsibility for the repair is mine as well.

Sure, I've been busy. Isn't everyone? The truth is I have overlooked these very important relationships with my horses in favor of other activities and priorities. Sometimes other responsibilities need our time, but we must make time to reflect on our important relationships. If we don't, we may find that time spent on other tasks has resulted in serious damage to the relationships we failed to maintain.

When we encounter the unexpected in relationships, what do we do? Do we shake our heads and wonder without ever reaching a thoughtful conclusion? Or do we think through the puzzle until we arrive at the correct explanation and establish a plan of action to polish the tarnish from the relationship?

Whether with a horse, human, or otherwise, be sure to make time to regularly reflect on your important relationships.

Reflection and Motivation

Any actions we take that are rooted in anger are guaranteed to damage our relationships. How often have you seen a horse owner react in anger to a horse that did not do as the person wanted? A voice is raised, a stick brandished, a whip is cracked, or a rein is jerked, bruising a tender mouth with the action of an iron bit. And to what purpose?

Why did the human react this way? What was his goal? Was that goal achieved? If some short term goal was achieved, what was sacrificed in the process? If you have ever found yourself in a similar place, angry and frustrated by the behavior of a child or horse, did you stop to reflect or did you just lose it?

Sure, there are examples of children or dogs that will try desperately to get closer to the one who has just raised a voice or fist. However, those sad attempts at relationship in no way lessen the truth that the displays of anger or violence are always detrimental to the relationships involved. All these tragic cases prove is that the victim (child or dog) was already severely damaged. No healthy psyche, human or canine, will run to violence; the healthy will always run away if that opportunity exists.

As mentioned a few paragraphs ago, it is better to react immediately to an error than to let it grow. In the case of Asti and her stable mates, I did act immediately. I did not act in anger. I wasn't angry. But I was highly disappointed—in myself.

Good horse trainers never stay in the company of their equine student when they experience anger or frustration. There were very few occasions where I had to leave the arena due to anger or frustration, but it did happen.

I well remember every horse that put me in that position: Billy, Lady J, Sneakers, and one sweet little pregnant POA mare. Her name escapes me because I was never mad at her, just baffled by her problem until I got it figured it out.

Whenever I ran into a real issue with a horse and realized I didn't have a logical next move, rather than simply reacting, I tied the horse up safely and securely as close as possible to where the incident occurred and left. In each of these instances I went up to the house, sat on the back porch and reflected. And reflected. A time or two I called a friend who had a lifetime of horse experience and talked through the problem. Like most wise counselors, she just steered my thinking until I arrived at clarity and a plan.

Each horse left my place with some degree of success—except Sneakers. He was able to be ridden when he left, but it was clear that our relationship was just not going to work out. I called his owner and told her to take him home. I remember well my words to her. "If I get on him one more time, I will shoot him." Sneakers not only had no ability, he had no interest whatsoever in relationship with me.

I could have gone the domination route with Sneakers, but the limited upside potential just didn't justify taking a course of action that might possibly hurt him or me. There are a lot of ways to make - or force - a horse do something. Nearly every one of them opens the door to potential injury or worse. It is always better to try to lead a horse through relationship, but there are cases where a horse just refuses to follow.

Success by using dominance in any relationship may make you the winner, but it also results in making the other party a loser. Valued relationships are always built on a win-

win formula. Worthy leadership begins with consideration for the one being led. Can you remember any instance where Jesus considered Himself the winner and we the losers? He is a Good Shepherd, the victor over death, not over His flock.

Relationships are like savings accounts. You can't keep making withdrawals unless you make frequent deposits. If you try, you will receive a big past–due notice right when you most need to make another withdrawal. The ponies and I will be spending more time together. I will return to making consistent deposits to properly balance our relationships. We will reestablish the habit of obedience, enhancing both their lives and mine.

How are your relationships doing? Are you simply doing tasks, or are you properly relating to children, staff, friends, and most importantly, to the Lord? Are the important relationships in your life getting stronger? Are you making regular deposits in each relationship account?

Build time into your busy life to reflect. Without regularly evaluating your most important relationships, you may discover them badly tarnished from neglect with no cushion left in your account. If you never allow time in your schedule for reflection, you may be surprised when you miss the fork in the road of relationship only to look back and wonder just where that fork was you should have taken.

If you always push forward and never stop to see where you are, you may not realize there was an option offered that you were too busy to even notice, much less consider. You miss some beautiful scenery along the way if you never take time to reflect; you may also miss a wonderful opportunity or even an answer to prayer. It was there, you just missed it in your complete busyness.

Simple Is Usually Best

Life decisions are seldom as complicated as we want to make them. Horses are used in ministry in large part because they are simple. Horses do not lie, rationalize, or complicate issues. They are direct and consistent. Horses teach us how to be simple as little children, for so we must be to enter the kingdom of heaven.

It is not part of the horse's nature, but part of human nature to take what is simple and make it so complicated that no computer could sort it out properly. The usually extensive list of options and scenarios we come up with for seemingly difficult problems are way too complex to wrap our head around. If some decision-computer assigned a probability factor to our list of possible actions, option A might be 80 percent likely to produce the result we seek; option B could be 68 percent likely to accomplish our goal, and so on. How can we be sure to pick the one that will deliver what we want?

Life is like an algebra problem; we get the right answer when we reduce it to its simplest form. Reflection provides an opportunity to take what appears to be a complicated question and reduce it to the simplest terms. Once the basics of the possible choices are set before us, picking the right decision is usually quite simple.

How many of us have had a commitment on our calendar when what seems like a golden opportunity appears that require us to decide whether to take it and cancel what is already booked or pass it off? Most of us, I bet. So, what do you do?

If after a month of evading the task of weeding the garden, you promise your wife that it would be done this coming Saturday and then you received an invitation to fill an unexpected opening in a golf tournament foursome, what would you do? What decision would your wife support? If the golfers are friends, you might be wise to weed the garden. If the invitation includes exclusive face time with the president of your company and this is potentially a major career opportunity, your wife might be more than happy to let the weeds grow and send you off with a big kiss of support.

Choosing to golf with friends may break a commitment made to your wife. Should your wife consider this Saturday a metaphorical line in the sand testing whether you will ever keep your word to her again, then the whole job thing is of little importance if you fail to follow through. But, if your wife is absolutely giddy with the prospect of you spending time with the big boss, then you have not broken a promise.

The equation must be reduced to one of commitment. Who did I make the commitment to? Once you answer that question, if the opportunity presented still seems to be overwhelmingly attractive, let the one to whom the commitment was made decide. It's as simple as that. While the decision itself may seem to be of little significance, you nevertheless testify to your character, honor, and faith by the action you take.

As leaders of our children, horses, community, classroom, or employees, each decision we make either reinforces the faith and trust placed in us or damages it when we fail to make decisions worthy of the leader we say we are. Leaders never take vacations. Parents never take vacations. God never takes vacations.

" But let your 'Yes' be 'Yes,' and your 'No,' 'No.' For whatever is more than these is from the evil one. "

- Matthew 5:37

So, why don't people just get simple and make reasoned decisions? The answer is usually related to the lack of the one perfect outcome on their list of options. We want something that just isn't offered. Have you ever just kept chewing on a problem because you want what you want and not what is possible, rather than making a decision and moving forward?

The Holy Spirit can't work with us when we are caught up in some logic-based or complex computation of vision. Faith is not logical or complex. Only by getting simple are we able to hear and see what the Spirit brings to us.

Make time to reflect. Know what the options truly are before making any decision. Reduce the question to its simplest form. Are you really deciding between weeding and golfing? Or is the choice far more important; a few hours of fun or failing to honor a commitment made to your life partner?

Is there anything you are choosing over your commitment to Jesus Christ? You can only arrive at a truthful answer by reflecting in the simple light of the Spirit.

COMMITMENT

There is a consistency and common truth found in most earthly things like cycles of life, nature, and society. No matter what we come up with that takes us on a detour away from the basic truths of God, circumstances will eventually correct themselves (or will be corrected!) to line up more closely with the original order of things and restore some semblance of balance.

One example of this is the all-around horse. When man and horse first entered into relationship there were no specialties. Horses packed, dragged, and carried. They were ridden, used for transporting goods, hitched to wagons, sleighs, and farm implements. In Arabia, the most highly prized mares shared the tents of the humans and the children were fed mare's milk.

Interestingly enough, as I write these words, articles about a return to favor of the all-around horse are beginning to appear in horse journals. There have been only a few so far, but the tide will be coming in as the horse market begins to reflect this shift in horse values. Since Christians do not believe in coincidence, the trend for many of the faithful to once again consider what God says to be more important than what some preacher on TV says is part and parcel of the same phenomena. We are beginning to recognize that God's plan is superior in every respect to our own.

It has been a number of decades since the all-around horse was king. The horse most highly prized was the one who was willing and able to serve his owner as a work horse, companion, baby-sitter, and show horse. Life was good for both horse and human then. Relationship was important.

If you think about it for a moment, the same was true of human society. Farmers produced most of what they needed and sold the excess for money to purchase what they could not make themselves. Women cooked, sewed, gardened, raised children, taught lessons, and epitomized the qualities of neighborliness when needed.

Men knew the basics of carpentry, animal husbandry, farming, mechanics, and most faithfully led their families, their congregations, and their communities. How many men or women do you know who could step into such shoes today and get the job done? Society has been devaluing the workhorses of the world, whether equine or human, for decades. What is most highly regarded today is the star. Most children today don't aspire to be great parents, teachers, police officers, or nurses, but rock stars, pro-athletes, moguls, and video wunderkinds—anything that puts them on center stage. The yardstick by which all value is now measured is celebrity and cash.

Once Ace and Shiner came home, I had to consider just what I was going to do with them. Did they return to us to be pets or to be trained to compete at the levels they were bred to achieve? What was my responsibility? Both Shiner and Ace should have the aptitude to excel in many disciplines, and I have the ability to make them into "something." But what would it take? Ace and Shiner weren't colts anymore; they were mature horses without skills. And isn't the value of a horse based upon utility? What kind of a challenge had I stepped into?

Where Did Commitment Go?

The economies of both the world and the United States have greatly changed in the past couple of years. Equine markets have tumbled as a result of over breeding, over specialization, the slaughter ban, and the continuing evaporation of the vast ocean of money that is needed to fund very expensive horse activities.

The disastrous conditions experienced by many horses and their owners are exacerbated by urban sprawl and the disappearance of relationship. Fewer folks have a place to keep horses at home, and most of the youth involved with horses today learn equitation skills but not relationship skills. It takes commitment to find success in relationship with a horse. Commitment is becoming more difficult to find.

It was this same lack of commitment that led to the sorry state of affairs for both Ace and Shiner. The family who bought them from us had boys, pasture, a love of horses, and the ability to support a horse habit. Well, things change. Kids get older and employment situations often cause families to reshuffle the deck. Ace and Shiner moved on.

There are thousands of wonderful, useful horses available across the United States for little to no money. Many will not find homes. It is easy to understand why the lady who had Ace and Shiner when we found them was not committed to their rescue. Why commit to a problem horse when there are so many better ones to choose from? Horses are disposable. Most folks say, "If I'm not completely happy with the one I have, I'll get another." Children are

[85]

disposable. "If my kids disappoint me or I remarry, I can always have more." Marriages are disposable. The "till death do us part" thing is only words, right? There's always another fish in the sea...

For more than twenty years I have been telling folks that they can have a horse or they can have a life; they can't have both. Most youth today are into sports, consumption, and technology. They have no time or interest in settling into the day-after-day needs, responsibilities, and rhythms of horse keeping.

The value of the all-around horse is rising in horse markets once again. Lack of time and funds have made the jack-of-all trades much more appealing than the once-prized master of only one. Perhaps the return of the all-around horse is also the result of recognizing that the barren places in our lives can only be filled by relationships. The sum of many piecemeal relationships will never add up to that of one meaningful relationship.

To save our society, our families, and our horses, we need to return to a focus on relationships. Anything of true worth is always somehow tied to a relationship. Our work should begin with those that are most important to us. Begin your work with your relationship with Jesus Christ. In that relationship you will find the perfect model of commitment.

Relationship Is the Prize

Every time I think about our six horses that need work and the time it would take to achieve a level of training to make each of them commercially valuable, I am simply overwhelmed. There is no way I can do it. I don't have the physical stamina or enough hours in the day to give each of them what is needed.

Let's begin with Shiner. After giving the question due consideration, I realized that he doesn't need to become a specialized show horse. He did not return to us to perform or be judged by a third party. Shiner is one of our own and that *is* his value, nothing more than just being one of our beloved horses. Shiner could easily be competitive in a number of disciplines. He has beautiful self-carriage and a lovely, deep stride. But competitive performance is not a requirement of our relationship.

Being blessed with a magnificent singing voice does not mean one is required to pursue singing as a profession. I can't sing, but it seems like a good illustration. Just because Shiner could be a show horse does not mean I am required to make one out of him. Enjoy your talents, be blessed by them, and bless others. If you love to sing, just sing. I will enjoy Shiner's talents even if no one else ever watches.

Gifts do not come with strings attached. Gifts do not obligate. Just because we *can* doesn't mean we *must*. Sure, there's reciprocity in any relationship. One characteristic of wonderful relationships, however, is the free offering of our gifts to each other. God gives us wonderful things because He loves us. There is no quid-pro-quo or balance sheet kept to be sure we get as much as we give.

With the limited time I have available for my horses, I would be a miserable failure indeed if I tried to make Shiner fit any pre-conceived mold other than beloved equine companion. My only goal with Shiner is to establish a proper relationship between us and enjoy both the process and the result. Beloved children of God are not required to compete either. Victory is ours by relationship with Jesus Christ. He did the work. He called us. All He needs from us is our commitment to the relationship.

[87]

Shiner need only be concerned about relationship with me. He doesn't have to worry about being a champion. Everything he needs I will provide. As our relationship develops he is learning to have faith and confidence in me as his leader. Most rewards of the pursuit of relationship are found in the journey itself.

As a chosen child of God, one for whom there is a nameplate on the door of your heavenly mansion, your highest value is not in celebrity or wealth, but the family relationship we share as children of God and heirs to His kingdom. His commitment to us was unto death. What is your commitment to Him?

FAMILY RESEMBLANCE

Should a knowledgeable horseman compare Ace and Shiner physically, he would probably never guess they were so closely related. There are precious few similarities that even an educated eye could see. The view when seen through spirit eyes is, however, vastly different.

Even though I knew and loved Ace and Shiner's sire and their mothers, even I don't see many common physical, or even emotional, traits that they share. I can, however, see many of their father's characteristics in each of them. While their family resemblance to each other isn't obvious, the family relationship they have to Sky certainly is. One reason I am sure of their parentage (aside from the fact that I bred and foaled them) is that I knew their father so well.

Shiner and I have been working on relationship while Ace is spending most of his time so far with Asti, just being a pasture pet until a stall opens and his turn comes. Asti is our elegant, black mare, sixteen hands of gleaming, black body decorated with white socks, a white blaze, and one cornflower-blue eye.

Shiner has also inherited much that I recognize from his mother, Scotch, as well. It is a far greater privilege to have this opportunity to learn more about Shiner's spirit than simply knowing what he grew to look like as a mature horse.

[89]

When I look at Ace and Shiner, I see many physical characteristics they share. Both have Sky's eye, similar in shape as well as possessing a similar expression. At odd moments when I look into Ace or Shiner's eyes, I almost feel like Sky is looking out at me from wherever he is, sharing part of his spirit with me through his sons.

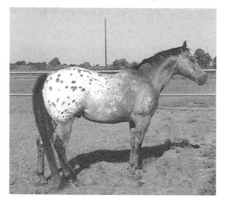

The last photo of Sky.

Both Ace and Shiner have great bone, dense and solid, with sturdy canons and great hocks. They also have correct legs, straight and clean. Ace and Shiner are both very athletic with powerful hindquarters and good, solid feet. Both Ace and Shiner have similar markings on their foreheads—symmetrical white stars.

Then there are the striking physical differences between them. Ace is a solid liver-chestnut, sporting a rich, deep, tobacco-brown coat that sparkles with a hint of gold when bits of sunlight catch the tips of his old, winter hair before reaching the newer, darker hairs of his short, finer summer coat. No passer-by would ever think Ace was an Appaloosa. He looks more like the Quarter Horses that appear in his extended pedigree than the highly colored Appaloosas in his ancestry.

Shiner, on the other extreme, is a bay roan with a gleaming-white blanket that begins just past his withers and continues over his hip and nearly down to his hocks. There are a few dark brown spots in an otherwise clear blanket of white. Shiner's legs are roan, a combination of dark brown and white hair. Where Ace has a longer, more elegant look, Shiner is short-coupled and compact. Ace has a thick mane and full, flowing tail that could easily drag the ground. Shiner has a thin mane and thinner tail. Both his mane and tail have grown since he's been with us, but Shiner will never be able to boast of a luxurious mane and tail like his brother.

Shiner seems to notice everything! Ace can be a bit aloof. Ace began as the leader outside the pasture; Shiner has more confidence than Ace in the pasture, though less so when people are involved. Shiner moves in a more upright frame, like a dressage horse or jumper. Ace moves long and low like a pleasure or hunt seat horse.

Ace seems to be very like his mother, Julie; temperamental under saddle if he hasn't been properly asked and always willing to give an opinion. Mind you, this is only my first impression. Once Ace has had the opportunity to fully comprehend the offer I will make him, he may have a very different response. We've all heard of absolute reprobates who became inspirational figures after being tested. Ace is certainly no scoundrel, and sometimes early impressions aren't completely accurate.

Shiner is like his mother, Scotch, solid and willing, but he has a difficult time concentrating for extended periods of time. And, while he is as honest as can be, he does have just a hint of his daddy's inclination to offer an opinion—but unlike Ace, Shiner never presses the point.

God's many children come in an endless variety when viewed with natural eyes. Except for the similarities shared by all humans, there is just not much physically that gives a clue of our true family relationship as heirs to His kingdom. Shiner and Ace may not resemble each other, but they are legitimate offspring and sons of their father. The family relationship we share with our brothers and sisters in Christ is not distinguished by our resemblance to each other, but by the characteristics of our Father that are evident in each of his children. When one is intimately acquainted with the Father and gifted with Spirit eyes, the family resemblance is unmistakable.

UNDAUNTED

Like horses, humans have both a thinking side and a reacting side. And also like the noble horse, we humans have an innate response system of fight-or-flight built into our basic makeup. Does this mean we are destined to always be fearful and flighty, just waiting for the opportunity to be spooked or panicked? Absolutely not.

The Christian mind is actually different from the non-Christian mind. The Christian mind I refer to here is one in right relationship with God. Christians who walk with the Lord truly live as if on another plane of existence. The new nature we receive through His Spirit elevates us above this two-dimensional world to a place of far greater vision.

How might this vision express itself? Many who walk according to the flesh may consider a dark cloud on the horizon as a cause for trepidation and fear of an impending storm. Those who walk in the spirit may have a greater vision, not seeing a threat or picture of gloom, but instead as a display of the majesty of God. One the one hand, if this dark cloud brings rain, it is a blessing to the land and what lives upon it. On the other hand, should the cloud merely roil in the heavens and the wind blow without rain, it is comforting evidence of the power of the Lord as He moves things about.

Or, perhaps it is a reminder that we often bring disharmony and strife to other lives without any upside of blessed change. Like a cloud without rain, sometimes we posture and crow without as much as laying an egg for breakfast.

"These men are blemishes at your love feasts, eating with you without the slightest qualm—shepherds who feed only themselves. They are clouds without rain, blown along by the wind; autumn trees, without fruit and uprooted—twice dead." -- Jude 1:12

As the dawn breaks, whether it brings brilliant sun or shaded skies, it is only our human interpretation that assigns it some arbitrary value of being good or bad. If it is bright, are we pleased or discouraged? It depends on what we want at the moment: clear weather for a morning ride across the pastures or thick clouds offering the possibility of rain to parched ground.

If the day begins with a thick, gray veil, only our emotion and prejudice will judge the weather to be gloomy and dreary. I would prefer to think of such a dark, cottony, cuddly sky as an opportunity to reflect on the glory and grace of God over a hot cup of coffee or tea. If time does not permit coffee, it is still a blessing and delight to be able to spend the morning learning with my horses without having to smear thick greasy sun block all over my face and arms!

Do you see that there is no particular mood attached to either the weather or the day except as defined by our preconceptions? Such judgments are arbitrary. Some people just seem to have a more negative vision than others. The closer our vision aligns with that of our Savior, the more positive our outlook will become. Human nature can change just as much as a horse's nature can change.

Is a Quarter Horse better than an Appaloosa? That would mean that Bo, one of my amazing grays, is better than Shiner. Is our sixteen-hand mare better than the fourteen-hand filly? That would mean that elegant Asti is better than my other amazing gray, little Swizzle. Is a beautiful, dangerous horse better than one who has slim pickin's in the looks department but is as honest and reliable as the day is long?

Looking only at the canvas of appearance, it is impossible to answer such one-dimensional questions properly. Why do we let meaningless criteria limit our delight in the day God provides for us each morning? In Romans 8:5, Paul tells us, *"Those who live according to the flesh set their minds on the things of the flesh, but those who live according to the Spirit, the things of the Spirit."*

The mind and vision of the Spirit lifts us far above this flat world occupied by those who live solely by the flesh, by nature alone, without the divine breath of God to inspire them. Do you find yourself limited, living in a two-dimensional plane, subject to whatever the day brings? Or are you ready to accept the life and limitless vision offered by the Spirit of the Lord?

Do you want to ride a trail pony that only knows how to follow the tail in front of its nose, or do you want to ride free across the mountaintops as the breezes of possibility blow silky mane hair onto your outstretched hands? Just like the rider who is freed from the bonds of earth by the strength of his horse, so we as children of God are not shackled by the chains that bind and convict those who live solely by the flesh.

People who do not hear the Shepherd's voice are left to aimlessly roll about the landscape as best they can, subject to the whims of other men and the ever-changing statutes of local and national governance. These who are lost are never content, never satisfied; they have a thirst that is unquenchable. They are without Jesus Christ.

Shiner and Ace thought they had been abandoned; sentenced to spend their few remaining days in that dry, dusty, hot, and hopeless pasture in northern Texas. Now home again, their spirits have returned and their vision expands as the dimensions of relationship with us bring new hope and security. The hot times of their past are gone. Certainly the summer heat will return each year, but Ace and Shiner will never again look at the weather as anything but the decoration of the day or assign to it any importance whatsoever.

As a chosen member of the family of Jesus Christ, are you experiencing the new vision of the Spirit? Because you are free of the law of sin and death you should no longer look at the sun as either punitive or healing, but as evidence of the power and sovereignty of God.

Relationship to Jesus Christ offers you a far greater vision. That vision brings blessings of security, purpose, and peace. Refuse to be confined, convicted, or limited by random conditions or circumstances. You are a child of the King.

"To be carnally minded is death, but to be spiritually minded is life and peace. For you did not receive the spirit of bondage again to fear, but you received the Spirit of adoption..." -- Romans 8:6, 15

A particular set of circumstances may cause the reacting side of a horse's personality or the natural mind of the human to react in fear, to run or fight for their lives. In contrast, however, the secure horse, the secure Christian, may not even acknowledge that same stressor as being anything of great concern at all. Horses and humans who trust their leader with their very lives are never distressed.

When Ace first saw our horse trailer, he was certain he was not going to get into it. Ace was using the reacting side of his brain and tried to escape his fear of the trailer by running backward, rearing up, and attempting to flee the scene. Once Ace learned to trust me, the thinking side of his brain switched on and he began to load up without fear. Ace went from *dis*tress to *no* stress.

Christians may be fully aware of what appear to be critical issues and challenges, but we evaluate those circumstances by looking to God for direction. In such a situation, the Christian is not *unaware*; the Christian is *undaunted*.

Confident horses and secure Christians seldom react in fear; they are conditioned by relationship to use the thinking side of their personality. We consider, we process, and we rely upon our confidence in our leader. God is responsible for those really big things.

"I'm Good with That"

When an event that might spook a "natural" horse happens to one of mine, he should look to me to see if there is any need for concern. Once assured that "No, all is well," he should be able to say to himself, "I'm good with that" and return to whatever he was doing before.

Economic, societal, health, and weather-related conditions cause natural humans to fret, fear, and lather at the peril of the times. Christians simply look to the Lord and ask, "Should I be concerned?" He will assert His calm Spirit in us and say, "No, all is well." We may then say to ourselves, "I'm good with that," and return, satisfied and secure, to whatever we were doing before.

As a horse trainer, I am responsible for making the big decisions. My horses are calm because I am calm. Christians are secure because our God is secure. Ace and Shiner rest peacefully, knowing they are safe. Christians are blessed to settle peacefully into their pillows at the end of each day, knowing that God has taken the night watch.

"Who (or what) shall separate us from the love of Christ? Shall tribulation, or distress, or persecution, or famine, or nakedness, or peril, or sword? Yet in all these things we are more than conquerors through Him who loved us."

-- Romans 8:35,37

My husband was diagnosed with stage-four colon cancer in 1986. Was that a stressor? Well, of course it was. Did it cause *dis*tress? No. When we looked to God's throne, He was still there and we were confident in relationship with Him. In similar circumstances, could you look to the Lord, receive reassurance, and say to yourself, "I'm good with that"?

Many geographic areas in the United States experience severe storms. As you sit with your family under the stairs to ride out the tornado marching through your area, can you look to the Lord, receive reassurance, and say to yourself, "I'm good with that"?

Can you think of any instance where God might respond to your request for reassurance and say, "You better worry now—I can't handle this one"? It is not possible for the God who spoke the world into existence to be stymied by anything some human can throw at Him. Don't fret about the weather, God made weather. Don't fret about earthquakes, God has been known to use earthquakes to do His bidding.

The proof of Paul's message, that we are more than conquerors through Jesus Christ, plays out daily in the Christian body by the power, comfort, and peace that relationship with Christ offers us. This peace is one of the strongest evangelical tools Christians have to impact non-believers.

A horse securely bonded to its trainer/leader will not exhibit the same fight-or-flight response as a horse without such relationship. The bonded horse doesn't even have to be with its trainer to be exempt from concern about a situation that might cause panic in another horse. The mind of a horse in right relationship with its master is actually different from that of the natural horse without the security of such relationship. We become New Creations through relationship with Jesus Christ. My horses are new creations through relationship with me. The Ace that calmly stepped up into the horse trailer with me was evidence that he could become a new creation.

Can you say the same for yourself? For your children?

Christians live in a completely different reality from non-Christians. We are different. We are never abandoned to fend for ourselves once Christ has claimed us. All that matters is the relationship; cancer, weather, and everything else simply describe our circumstances of the moment. Shiner and Ace will never again be abandoned or left to fend for themselves. They have been redeemed.

Perfect Provision

When I walked back to the house in the damp, cutting wind in the dark that New Year's Eve, I was overcome with gratitude that I belong to God. The horses galloped up to the barn when I called them in to supper and a night's sleep in their warm deeply-bedded stalls. They had obviously been waiting for the opportunity!

Watching the four head toward the barn was more like watching a stampede than hungry ponies called in to dinner. Not a one of them governed down their speed as they got closer and closer to their gates. My little darlin's had to make some fairly creative and athletic moves in order to get slowed down enough to zip into their houses without running into the gate or me. Usually I don't allow such wild behavior, but tonight I let them come in at a run.

Did my horses earn their feed today? If you mean, "Did they work for their room and board today?" the answer is no. I have requirements and expectations, of course, but such basics are never withheld due to lack of performance.

"Which of you, if his son asks for bread, will give him a stone? If you, then, though you are evil, know how to give good gifts to your children, how much more will your Father in heaven give good gifts to those who ask Him!"

-- Matthew 7:9,11

My role as a horse-keeper is one I relish. I delight in providing quality food, water, shelter, and bedding for all our horses. As a small treat for everyone (including me), I took a little extra time with each horse that night, currying winter coats before tucking each one in.

Is there a quid pro quo with God when it comes to our daily provisions? No. Our Father would no more withhold our daily bread because we did not work for it today than I would keep my horses gazing wistfully at an empty feeder. Daily bread isn't just the stuff with wheat and food value. Daily bread is everything we need for each 24 hour period, whether physical, spiritual, or emotional.

Ace and Shiner know what it's like to have food withheld unless they are called up to work. That was when they were far from home, but no longer. Now they are home, cared for in our family even as I am cared for by my Father. Ace and Shiner don't always get to set the menu, but they will always receive everything they need, as will I.

All we have belongs to God. All that ever *was* belongs to God. All that will ever *be* belongs to God. In truth, the richest king or wealthiest nation owns nothing. Earthly wealth is just a silly game of temporal Monopoly. God holds the only bank with any true assets, and in any contest, His bank will always win. It already has.

Every pantry is stocked with the goods of God. Every storehouse holds His bounty. As beloved children and heirs of the Kingdom, we are showered with blessings of God's riches every day.

We belong to Him and He cares for us just as I do my own beloved horses. Mature Christians receive all the spiritual gifts promised through relationship with Jesus Christ. We are peaceful, secure, joyful, and carry an easy burden. Oh, and let's not forget that mansion in eternity reserved exclusively for us when it is needed.

He Came Looking for Me

FAITH–HOPE–LOVE

"With us now abide faith, hope, love... but the greatest of these is love." -- 1 Corinthians 13:13

Together, these three comprise a complete overview of the Bible itself. One of our church elders presented a message recently about two twin brothers, Hope and Trust. His words inspired me to consider two other members of the same family, Faith and Love.

Faith

Righteousness was credited to Abraham by faith. God's promise is as relevant today as it was in Abraham's time. As was Abraham, we too are credited with righteousness by faith. But what is faith?

Christian faith believes that the God of the Bible is who He says He is, can do what He says He can do, and will do everything He promised. This is the same definition of faith I use when establishing the foundation of relationship with a horse. I strive to prove that I am who I say I am, can do what I say I can do, and will keep every promise. While my goal is to never disappoint, there will be times when I am imperfect in my execution of leadership. There will never be a time when God is not perfect in His.

It was Abraham's faith that made him willing to sacrifice his only son, Isaac. Abraham believed that God

[103]

could and would do as he promised. Abraham had faith that God would raise up even a dead son to be the father of the nations because that was the promise He made.

"The word of the Lord came to him... a son of your own body will be your heir. Look up at the heavens and count the stars—if indeed you can count them. So shall your offspring be...Abraham believed the Lord, and he credited it to him as righteousness." -- Genesis 15:4-6

My horses must have faith that I will live up to the promises I make to them as we build relationship and they begin to trust me as their leader. Ace and Shiner came to us with faith in nothing more than the bond of brothers who had never been separated.

Every moment I am with Ace or Shiner, I work to reinforce the glimmer of confidence, of faith, that they have in me as their herd leader. I have shown them who I am, convinced them that I have material power over their lives, and act in a way that will be consistent and faithful to do all that I promise to do. Which of us came to Christ unbroken? Ace and Shiner were without hope when they came home. They were broken spirits, without reserve and without strength. God is always faithful and well able to heal our broken places, and I must work very hard to be sure and deliver all that I promise Shiner and Ace.

In any leader-follower relationship, the concept of faith must enter into the equation. Whatever the leader promises must be delivered—each and every time. Of utmost importance to a follower is faith in the character and constancy of the leader. There are no vacations for effective leaders, parents, teachers, or horse trainers.

Faith is what neutralizes fear. How much faith does your horse have in you? How much faith do your children have in you?

Most horse fatalities in burning barns are caused when a horse refuses to leave the safety of its familiar stall. People may attempt to lead the panicked horse through the burning barn to safety, but the horse refuses to follow and the would-be rescuer must abandon the horse to save his or her own life. The fire generated more fear than the doomed horse had faith in the one who tried to lead it out of the barn.

"Faith never knows where it is being led, but it knows and loves the One who is leading." -- Oswald Chambers

Does your horse have more faith in you than it would fear of fire? How about your kids? Hopefully, you will never have an answer to that question by experience. How important is relationship? How important is faith? For our horses and our children, it can be a matter of life and death.

Once our relationship is firmly established, Shiner and Ace will ignore what might have previously caused them to run off in panic. They will choose instead to look to me for my reaction, believing that I have everything under control. They must have faith that I am who I said I am and that I both can and will do all that I promise. Only in such faith would they follow me out of a burning barn. In the odd instance where I might fall short, please don't tell them!

Faith allowed Abraham to raise the knife above a bound Isaac. The faith Abraham had in God exceeded the fear of losing his only son. Without faith, we cannot have a relationship with the God of the Bible and our savior, Jesus Christ. By faith we have confidence He will never fall short.

Hope

Ace and Shiner had no hope as they baked under the hot Texas sun before we arrived. They had no hope because they had no faith. They were horses alone, or so they thought.

Yet, today they are safe. They are loved. They are home.

The hope of salvation appears first in the book of Genesis and was the primary message of Old Testament prophets. Our hope today rests in the person of the Messiah, the Lord Jesus Christ. In Romans 8, we read that "Hope that is seen is no hope at all. Who hopes for what he already has? And while we hope for what we do not yet have, we wait for it patiently." *Faith is the father of Hope.*

Think about the many great, epic romances from literature, the silver screen, and real life: Cyrano and Roxanne, Lauren Bacall and Humphrey Bogart, Anthony and Cleopatra, Cosette and Marius from *Les Miserables*, Jane Eyre and Mr. Rochester, Jacob and Rachel, or Beauty and the Beast. It is the power of the relationship between the principals that is unique to these stories, not any beauty of face or circumstance. Frankly, in many such epics, one or both of the partners is quite plain or even hideous when seen by eyes not focused by love.

In nearly every case, the two lovers face what appear to be insurmountable trials: famine, fire, war, illness, separation; yet the love between each pair grows in spite of their circumstances. A constant in each of these relationships is the faith that begat a hope for the future, regardless of what tragedies are experienced in their present.

Happily ever after is a fairy tale. Surviving trial and separation, remaining true to love and to each other come what may is what elevates such romances to epic proportions. Faith is hope that has been tested and proved to be true.

Abraham waited a long time for the fulfillment of the promise God made that he would have descendents of his own body. Faith was enough to both sustain Abraham in the interim and to be the very vehicle by which the promise was kept. Is there a better tale of epic love than that between God and His children?

"But those who hope in the Lord will renew their strength. They will soar on wings like eagles; they will run and not grow weary, they will walk and not be faint." -- Isaiah 40:31

Our hope for passage through the narrow gate of Matthew 7:13 is in the person of Jesus Christ. Entrance is guaranteed through our faith and hope in His finished work on the cross.

Love

Even as faith begat hope, so the fulfillment of that hope is love.

"Love is patient, love is kind. It does not envy, it does not boast, it is not proud.

It is not rude, it is not self-seeking, it is not easily angered, it keeps no record of wrongs.

Love does not delight in evil but rejoices with the truth.

It always protects, always trusts, always hopes, always perseveres.

Love never fails. But where there are prophecies, they will cease; where there are tongues, they will be stilled; where there is knowledge, it will pass away.

For we know in part and we prophesy in part, but when perfection comes, the imperfect disappears.

When I was a child, I talked like a child, I thought like a child, I reasoned like a child. When I became a man, I put childish ways behind me.

Now we see but a poor reflection as in a mirror; then we shall see face to face. Now I know in part; then I shall know fully, even as I am fully known.

And now these three remain: faith, hope and love. But the greatest of these is love." -- 1 Corinthians 13:4-13

Consider the description of love contained in these oft-quoted verses from 1 Corinthians 13; do they not in every circumstance and particular describe both the Person and personality of our Lord?

Love is the person of Jesus Christ.

Faith is the work of the Holy Spirit.

Hope is the work of the human.

Love is the gift of the Father in Jesus Christ.

This concept is summed up in 1 Thessalonians 5: 8; "…let those of us who are of the day be sober, putting on the breastplate of faith and love, and as a helmet the hope of salvation."

Faith and love are visceral, covered by a breastplate that protects and encourages us through faith provided by the

Spirit and love in the person of Jesus Christ. Faith and love deliver body blows to an opponent when challenged. But Hope is very different from his brothers, Faith and Love. The helmet of hope covers the brain; the intellect that is ours to command.

"Now hope (what we know) does not disappoint, because the love of God (Jesus Christ) has been poured out in our hearts by the Holy Spirit (faith) who was given to us."

-- Romans 5:5

What standard do we attempt to attain as Christians? What is the gift available to each child of God? The gift is love. As you review each statement in these verses, you might recognize a benchmark against which you can properly evaluate every thought, action, or decision made ostensibly in the name of love.

Do you love your family? How well does your behavior stack up against these descriptions of love?

Do you love your horse? How does your behavior rate when compared to the true definition and practical description of love?

Do you love the Lord Jesus Christ? Again, on the scale provided by the author and true Person of love, do you honestly love, or are you simply whitewashing what is truly just a habit?

These three, faith, hope, and love, comprise a trilogy that is as impossible to separate as the Trinity itself. None may exist without the other.

When we went looking for Sky's sons we didn't realize that we would be bringing home the ones that natural eyes might consider the least lovely. The years Shiner and

Ace spent away from us held both physical and emotional hardship and their spirits were nearly extinguished by their circumstances.

Yet, like an epic romance, we have come together again. As the months pass, Shiner and Ace become more and more beautiful. If a movie were made chronicling the lives of Shiner and Ace, it would have a lovely beginning, a sad and sorrowful middle, and a great promise of a happy ending.

As my relationship with Shiner and Ace grows and strengthens, they are learning to have faith in my leadership, hope in my constancy and justice, and the ultimate reward will be the love we share.

"To love means loving the unlovable. To forgive means pardoning the unpardonable. Faith means believing the unbelievable. Hope means hoping when everything seems hopeless." -- G. K. Chesterton

[110]

Ace and Tantrums

Ace is the least dominant of any of our horses with the possible exception of thirty-year-old Sally. Ace had a severe head injury as a baby, and we always wondered what he would be like when he grew up. Now that he has returned home we will have the opportunity to find out.

In the contest for food Shiner is the dominant one, giving direction to Ace on where he may eat. Ace follows Shiner in the pasture. Ace does not seem to pay as much attention to his surroundings and the neighborhood like watchful, alert Shiner does. Ace is more tentative entering buildings and certainly more so as far as the horse trailer goes.

Asti and Swizzle lost their cozy stalls in the main barn to Ace and Shiner a few days ago in my preparations to offer relationship to the Appaloosa boys. Over time, we'll see just what they are willing to offer in return. Swizzle and Asti will benefit from their time out this winter, and it is high time the soon-to-be ten-year-old geldings have their relational aptitude tested.

Well. First impressions can be deceiving.

It appears Ace is not as quiet and docile at feeding time as I thought. Our normally quiet and peaceful barn was loudly disrupted the first morning when I went out to feed.

[111]

The other three geldings were attentive yet polite, waiting their turn for the pellets to reach their feeders.

Mr. Quiet and Docile was not so patient and not so quiet. Ace was slamming his right front hoof into the wooden stall wall with both rhythm and passion. How odd to have such behavior in my barn. The question came to mind, *Am I going to allow this behavior?* The obvious answer was, *No.*

Allowing a horse to throw a tantrum of any kind is both annoying to those in attendance and damaging to the balance, serenity, peace, and character of the horse itself. Ace banging his foot on the stall wall is the equivalent of a petulant child lying on the ground, kicking and flailing as he screams for attention.

Horses, like humans, do not throw tantrums out of strength, but out of weakness.

As the human who is offering leadership, security, and relationship to Ace, I am completely responsible to make him able to overcome the weakness that is the genesis of this feeding-time tantrum. We will never find right relationship with each other, and he will never develop boldness, if I cannot lead him to a place where tantrums are no longer in his bag of behaviors.

Lesson One

After feeding Bo, Copper, and Shiner, I prepared a bucket for Ace, set it outside his stall, and entered his door with nothing more than an eight-foot length of red, cotton rope in my hand named Ol' Red.

My red rope was originally a lead rope that had long ago lost its snap. I use it as a safety belt of sorts when

[112]

training without a halter, just to have something available in case I need to quickly gain control of an equine body part.

The exercise I used to quiet Ace in response to his mealtime anxiety (demands) is the same one I use to calm and re-center any horse who has already had the most basic education in my equine school of relationship; I control their feet.

After entering Ace's stall, I threw the red rope over his neck. My intention was to catch it by both ends around his neck and use it to suggest a turn of his body. His reaction was to scoot away from the rope as it came through the air at him. Well, that was not unexpected. At least he didn't rear, charge out the open, rear door of the stall, or have a severe reaction.

When Ace faced me again, I threw the red rope again. Again, he moved away, though at a considerably slower speed and with far less conviction. I walked up to him, rubbed his shoulder with the rope, and then popped it over his neck. Once the rope was in place, I went straight to the basics. I moved with intent toward Ace's hindquarters, asking him to soften, bend, and yield his hips away from me. He responded perfectly and I was in control of his feet.

Unlike humans, the two sides of a horse's brain do not speak to each other. One must consistently teach lessons on both sides of a horse since the left eye lives a life completely different from the right eye. Once Ace politely yielded his hips a few times each way, remaining perfectly still as I changed sides, I slipped the red rope off his neck.

As the other horses happily continued munching their breakfast, Ace now stood quietly with both of his eyes looking directly at me. I sent the red rope out into the air again on Ace's near side and draped it over his back. By the third toss, Ace stood completely still and began to relax. I stopped. A few seconds later, I tossed the rope across his back again while counting each toss aloud: 1…2…3…4. I continued pitching the red rope across Ace's hips and over his neck until he lowered his head and sighed.

Ol' Red and I went to Ace's other side and repeated the exercise until he was perfectly happy and content. It was time for step two. I picked up Ace's feed bucket from outside his stall and poured the pellets and oats into his feeder. Interestingly enough, Ace thought it was time to eat it and stepped past me to go to the feeder. His attention was drawn away from me. Unacceptable.

Back to the exercises we went. Yield hips, back away. Throw the red rope. Repeat. When Ace was content to stand without trying to inch his way over to the feeder and was willing to maintain his focus on me, I left the stall and headed back to the house.

Lesson Two

The next morning I went out to the barn to feed, wondering how Ace would behave. I was pleased that he was quiet. I considered whether another lesson was really necessary, then realized that it was laziness asking the question. I fed the other three and skipped Ace. His response was one little tap on the stall wall. Just as I reached his stall door with the feed bucket and the red rope, Ace's hoof rapped the stall wall one more time.

We repeated the entire lesson from the day before. And again, once Ace was content to wait for my next direction, even after the bucket was emptied into his feeder, the lesson ended. I left to go back in the house and start a second pot of coffee.

So far, I am hopeful that Ace is willing to be an attentive student. The barn is already much quieter. Tomorrow will be lesson number three.

Lesson Three

The next time I went out to feed, Ace did not even go near his stall wall, much less pound on it. Trying to be the faithful leader I promised Ace I am, I hesitated for only a moment before walking into his stall to reinforce the lesson of properly focused attention before filling his feeder.

Ace remembered his lessons. He remained focused on me from the time I entered the barn until I left his stall. "Nicely done, Mr. Ace," I said before returning to the house. With the consistent improvements Ace was making, I was feeling quite good about both our progress and the prognosis.

Lesson Four - It Always Gets Darker

So, what happened the next time I went out to the barn to feed? You know the saying, "It is always darkest just before the dawn"? Well, everyone knows that cliché because it is usually true. It was much darker in the barn this morning, and I am not referring to the amount of sun coming in the skylights and breezeway doors.

We seldom experience an evenly ascending learning curve in any pursuit. There will always be starts and stumbles, plateaus and slips, falls and failures before leaps and bounds. Today, Mr. Ace presented me with stumbles, slips, and failures.

[115]

"Most of the important things in the world have been accomplished by people who have kept on trying when there seemed to be no hope at all." -- Dale Carnegie

As I began measuring pellets into the four feed buckets Ace started pounding. He wasn't drumming the wall with quite his original passion, but the decibel level wasn't that much less either. I am well acquainted with the peaks and valleys of learning curves, so recognized it for what I hoped it was, just a routine speed bump on the road to victory.

Shiner was fed. Bo was fed. Copper was fed. Ace continued to pound on his stall wall. I believe Ace's brothers were just a bit annoyed by this rude interruption of their usually quiet mealtime. My reliable red rope came out of the tack room once again. I placed Ace's feed bucket outside the door to his stall and went in to begin lesson number four.

The drill was the same. Ace yielded his hindquarters. I backed him away from any movement toward the feeder. I threw Ol' Red at his back. He didn't care about that at all today, never making even the slightest move away as the rope pitched through the air at him.

Ace did seem to have a little issue when I sent the rope flying at his head from dead-center front. Well, most horses would. However, mine shouldn't. So the red rope made the journey to Ace's neck, ears, forehead, and muzzle over and over until his attention left the rope and returned to me.

It was more difficult today to get Ace's attention away from the corner of his stall where the feeder hangs and back onto me. So I added a new exercise, repeated all the others, and prepared to find an ending to the lesson. Rome wasn't built in a day, and a horse will not change a habit formed over years in just a few short lessons.

The goal of Ace's lessons is not just to rid the barn of his annoying noise; the goal is also to add more foundation to our relationship. This is where we add perseverance to the lesson plan.

"Count it all joy when you fall into various trials, knowing that the testing of your faith produces perseverance." -- James 1:2-3

"I know your works, love, service, faith, and your perseverance." -- Revelation 2:19

When I walk into the barn, I want each horse to place its complete attention on me. I want Ace to look at me and see what I am doing, to catch any cue, sound or movement that might relate to him. I do not want him to look to see where the food is. I want him to look for his leader.

Bad Behavior = Poor Relationship

Horses who behave badly at feeding time are demonstrating a problem in their relationship with their leader. The food is merely a catalyst or trigger and not the cause of the bad behavior. Many horses get pushy when the feed bucket arrives due to lack of work, a need for attention, or insufficient enforcement of rules. The time to address such disrespectful and potentially dangerous behavior is the *first* time it happens. Horses aren't aggressive because they are over confident; they are pushy because they are somehow unbalanced.

As we grow in our ability to properly lead our horses, we gain more understanding of what such negative behaviors actually mean. We must look beyond the visual (or noise) to see the true cause and design an appropriate plan to strengthen the relationship we have with our horse, with our children, with our employees, with one another.

When humans behave badly, it too is evidence of weakness in a relationship. The greater our concern and the higher the value we place on any particular relationship, the more we will look beyond simple behaviors and work to discover the actual cause of the poor behavior that we may address it practically. The greater the importance of a relationship, the greater the investment we are willing to make in repairing damaged places in the fabric of the relationship. Any poor behavior of our own is due to a weakness in our relationship with God. It doesn't matter if the behavior is in relation to another person, to an event, or to a circumstance. Any decision to act out or behave badly is always of our own making and generated from a need, and not a place of strength.

The good news is that perseverance and a correct lesson plan will eventually lift us out of the depths of the valley and return us to a higher place of positive change and improvement. Ace will get better. Remember, I am not working to correct a specific fault; I am making an investment in our relationship. Miracles do happen, but most relationships are forged from commitment and perseverance. Keep at it and your darkness will eventually brighten into glory.

"Many of life's failures are men who did not realize how close they were to success when they gave up."

- Thomas Edison

Will attention to relationship solve all behavioral problems? Unfortunately not. There are unbalanced humans who may struggle forever in a search for peace. Likewise, there are unbalanced horses that may respond to leadership but never connect all the dots and be able to build an unshakeable foundation. In most cases horses can achieve balance through consistent worthy leadership. Once established, however, this fragile place of contentment and security must be maintained on a daily basis.

I am convinced there is an intentional role for such individuals in the world. While I don't know what that role may be in most cases, there is One who does and who is forever faithful. Regardless of earthly challenges, relationship with Jesus Christ does offer a peace that passes our understanding that may soothe even the most unbalanced child.

"Therefore, having been justified by faith, we have peace with God through our Lord Jesus Christ, through whom also we have access by faith into this grace in which we stand ... And not only that, but we also glory in tribulations, knowing that tribulation produces perseverance; and perseverance, character; and character, hope. Now hope does not disappoint, because the love of God has been poured out in our hearts by the Holy Spirit who was given to us."

- Romans 5:1-5

TURNING UP THE FLAME

The short walk to the barn the following morning was chilly and damp. When precipitation is thin and whisper-soft, Baber and I describe it as "mistifying." Even though it was neither raining nor snowing, the toes of my ancient Uggs were soaked clear through by the time I got back to the house from the barn.

Ace had slid even a bit further down the scale of performance this morning. As soon as I went to the feed cart, his hooves began beating their passionate tattoo on the stall wall. If I were to acknowledge Ace's bad behavior by telling him to be quiet, I would then be required to take immediate action. The hoof-on-wall noise isn't the issue; the problem is Ace's lack of proper focus. Yelling at him wouldn't accomplish anything of value.

I completely ignored Ace until Shiner, Copper, and Bo were fed. Again, my red rope and I entered Ace's stall. Ace has already learned that I will be entering his stall, so he is waiting for me at the door rather than standing at his feeder in expectation. How interesting.

Is Ace's noisy demand changing from, "Feed me now" to "Get in here quickly so I can get to breakfast"?

Today's lesson revealed an Ace who is no longer afraid of the red rope. It can sail onto his back, wrap around his ears, twirl in the air, and he remains completely

[121]

unconcerned. It is time to turn up the heat a little. My student is beginning to lose his concentration. I need to get more creative before he does.

Establishing Leadership

Horses look at humans in one of three ways: as predators, members of the herd or of no consequence at all—like a rock. My goal is to be herd leader. I will be completely useless if Ace perceives me as a predator. He will ignore me if he thinks of me as if I were just part of the scenery. However, if I am his herd leader, he will learn to always keep one ear tuned toward me to see how he should react to every stimulus, whether it is my cue or some change in his environment.

Success will have Ace looking at the red rope as if it were of no more consequence than an old rock. We've pretty much got that foundation laid. Now I need to turn up the heat and get him a bit more invested in *me*. Ace started our lesson period today being about seventy-five percent attentive to my body language and verbal tone. That is far short of what I need in order to restructure our leader-follower relationship and bring Ace to a happy place where the mealtime drumbeat disappears.

The Proverbial reference to the "fear of God" as the beginning of wisdom comes to mind. One definition of fear is *respect*. We need to fully believe that God has a material influence on our life today and our life hereafter. Ace needs to completely, 100 percent, believe that I have a material influence on his life now and in the future. God will not settle for seventy-five percent and I won't either.

In *Amazing Grays, Amazing Grace,* I shared a very correct and concise description of leadership regarding horses and humans. It is Clinton Anderson who said, "He who controls the feet wins." I need to exhibit proof that I can control Ace's feet. This is where philosophy fades into the background and action must take center stage. There comes a time when we must claim our leadership position. The respect and authority that comes with leadership is never given to us; it is earned.

Earning Respect

Without a halter, using my body position alone, I asked Ace to yield his hindquarters. This time I wanted a faster, more precise response. That meant making a bigger, more insistent move toward his hip. Not surprisingly, he moved forward as if being driven and headed out the open door of his stall to the pen beyond.

As soon as Ace turned away from me, I got in behind him and got to work. The old red rope started twirling in the air behind him, lightly attacking his butt as he ran in front of me. The red rope kept after him until he had hustled back into his stall to where this little exercise began. My body direction again asked him to yield his hip. With head in the air, eyes wide, and nostrils flaring (and a tiny little snort), Ace complied—and with dispatch. I turned away to release the pressure, letting him know in horse language that he got the answer right.

As you already know, both sides of a horse need to be worked equally. So I repeated my request for Ace to cross his hind legs and move his hip away from me on the off side. Ace made a fairly nice, crisp response. Not bad.

Our level of respect for God escalates exponentially when He decides to grab our attention by using a big or noisy cue that even dull humans can't miss. The moment we exhibit the correct response, God gives us a break and loves on us a little. There is fear and then there is respect. I don't want Ace to be afraid of me; I want him to respect me. God doesn't want His children to be afraid of Him; He wants them to understand that He is in control. Respect is king. Remember, I don't want Ace to think of me as a predator; I want to be considered a trustworthy leader.

God is no more predatory than I am. He uses power judiciously and emphatically. Do I have the power of life and death over Ace? Certainly. Does God have the power of life and death over me? Absolutely. But I only use fear as a tool when necessary to make a point or grab attention that refuses to stop wandering. Fear is only properly applied when a horse has no fear to begin with. Horses without fear are usually spoiled rotten. When they behaved badly in the past they may have been threatened, smacked, or yelled at, but were never hurt or properly chastised. They know you don't mean what you say or that you'll never follow through with your threat. God always follows through and so do I.

Fear is a vehicle that is able to carry us to a new place where relationship may flourish. God never uses fear as His end game, and neither do I. But when a situation warrants, the tool box opens and fear comes out to do our bidding. Sometimes horse trainers, like God, have to use bigger and stronger cues to get the attention of the horse or human who isn't with the program. Once we begin to understand and respond correctly, God will give us a break and love on us a little—as will a good horse trainer.

So, I loved on Ace a little. I asked him to walk to me. I hugged his head, messed with his ears, and rubbed Ol' Red all over his head and neck. Then I asked him to back away one step. He did. Ace softened and began to hug me back.

But he still looked over at his feeder from time to time. That is not what I want. I need his complete attention. For the moment, I want 100 percent participation as long as I am in the stall with him. Eventually I hope to reflexively have his attention whenever he can see or hear me, regardless of his surroundings.

I asked Ace to yield his hindquarters again, and with some conviction. Again, he headed out the door of his stall to his pen. Ace either wants to escape or is seeing which of us can out-stubborn the other. The remedy is the same no matter which of those options is causing his behavior.

Ace's feet were moving so I took action to regain control of them. Ol' Red and I got in behind Ace again and strongly encouraged him to move faster. Red and I kept at it until Ace zipped back through the door and into his stall. I had Ace's complete attention for the moment. A few more requests to yield, a little more loving, and Ace was now ready for breakfast.

What did I learn? I learned that Ace is becoming less concerned about the little things that caused him to react in fear. Now I need to turn up the heat and lead him through the transition from reacting in panic and fear to moving as directed in obedience. Ace is in danger of becoming complacent. He's beginning to accept a new status quo. He is still task oriented. The secret to moving him from task orientation to a habit of obedience is by demonstrating my power to control where and when his feet move.

There is always another lesson to teach our horse. There is always another lesson that God has in mind for us. We will never graduate on this side of the narrow gate. We only stop learning if *we* decide to drop out. What message would I be sending Ace if I decided to quit and just let him

[125]

bang the stall wall? I would be reinforcing his lack of faith in my authority. I would have lied to him. I won't do it. So, we will continue his lessons.

As Scarlet O'Hara said in *Gone With the Wind*, "Tomorrow is another day." I look forward to lesson number five with Ace.

Ace the Homeless

There are some homeless people who are homeless as a result of circumstance, while others are homeless by choice. I am beginning to wonder if Ace isn't like those folks who prefer to be out in the open, more comfortable without the safety and security of hearth and home.

Shiner is in a state of transition. Ace and Shiner are one week apart in age. Neither has ever known a world without the other. Shiner appears to welcome the opportunity to join the family. Ace, not so much. Ace is as friendly as they come, but his thought process so far is very odd for a horse.

Copper and Bo were in place this evening, standing out in the pasture waiting for me to show up. I did, and so did they. They went politely to their respective stall gates and in for dinner they came. Shiner and Ace had been up by the barn before I got there, but ran off again almost immediately. Ace hugs the cross fence and Shiner clings to him for company when Ace's behavior makes him start to feel insecure.

After being called a couple of times, Ace came trotting up with Shiner following close behind. I opened Ace's pen gate wide—but he didn't go in. He stopped, looked at the opening, considered, then turned and ran off to the fence line three hundred feet away. Shiner kept on

[126]

coming and waited for me to open his gate. Shiner walked into his house and went straight to his feeder.

Ace stayed at the fence line, looking over the top rail to see where Asti and Swizzle were. Shiner hollered out to Ace from the barn a time or two between mouthfuls, but quickly gave up to concentrate on his dinner. I decided I was going to help Shiner make the transition from being strictly Ace's brother to being part of the herd. I moved him from the end stall where his only neighbor was Ace to the stall between Ace and Bo. Ace would now have the end stall, leaving him with only Shiner for company.

Ace remained in the pasture. He ran run up to the barn a time or two after I called the horses in. Then almost immediately, he ran back out to the fence line again. I was certainly not going to hang around to open the stall gate whenever Ace finds it convenient.

Leaders lead and followers follow. I set the rules, not Ace. He may just have to spend the night outside. He has shelter, grass, water, and can stand next to the other geldings if he wants to. Dinner was served and everybody got tucked in for the night. Ace had his chance.

Abandoned by Choice?

Ace always shows up. He's always ready for a pet. He's willing, but only to a certain point. There is no abandonment yet. He is still homeless.

"The horse who abandons to the trainer asks no more "why" questions. The relationship the trainer has created with the horse firmly establishes the habit of obedience. Horses love routine and are concerned mainly about food, water, shelter, rest, and relationship with herd mates. Horses play and are inquisitive. Some horses have a low boredom

[127]

threshold; some are stodgy and a bit obtuse, but all horses must have a leader in order to feel secure. Are we as humans really much different? Only in abandonment to God are we certain never to be abandoned."

-- *Amazing Grays, Amazing Grace*

Is Ace just one of those individuals who prefer to be homeless? All the lessons and benefits of relationship will be offered to him. But whether or not he reciprocates by making a commitment of his own, only time will tell.

God offers each of us all of the lessons and benefits of relationship with Him. Folks who refuse to make a commitment to that relationship will find themselves eternally homeless. By relationship and kinship to Jesus Christ, our names appeared on His list. None will be lost and every child of the King will eventually enter the mansion He prepared particularly for them. Ours is both a present and a future of eternal love.

HERDSHIP

Shiner and Ace felt far, far removed from their home pasture when we found them. They felt abandoned and bereft. They were defeated.

But behind the scenes, God was at work. When the time was ripe, we were sent to look for them. Why? Certainly it was part of God's plan for Shiner and Ace, but the true purpose was to send a message of reassurance to all of His children. You're reading the message right this minute. You will not be lost. None will be lost.

Sometimes the messages we share with others hit home, especially those that originate with the Lord because the message speaks from His Spirit without to His Spirit within. Such messages often change our vision and change our lives. A lady at church recently told me how much the messages of *Amazing Grays* meant to her. She asked if she could come out to meet Bo and Swizzle, my two amazing gray horses.

"I feel like I already know them," she said.

Knowing that my words had found a home with another reader was music to my ears. I was quick to say that of course, she should come to meet the grays. The only experience this lady had with horses before reading the book was watching them from across the fence she shared with her neighbors. "The horses are so beautiful," was what she originally told me. Today she felt only sadness for these same "beautiful" horses.

"They have no relationship with the owners," she said. "They are just left out there by themselves without the owners giving them any attention at all. They have just been abandoned." I asked a few more questions and discovered that these six horses had adequate food and water. More importantly, they had herdship. While these horses weren't blessed with a relationship with their owners, at least they had each other. It could be far worse.

Before she learned how horses think and relate with one another, this lady saw the beauty of horses as simply one of God's creations. Indeed, horses are one of the most magnificent and noble animals we have been blessed to share our earth with. However, with her new understanding of the needs of a horse, the view across her lawn to the horses beyond had changed radically in her eyes. No longer did she have just a simple two-dimensional picture of horses. There was now the realization of what was lacking in their lives.

How often has a first impression later proven to be a false one? Do the pampered, rich celebrities we see on television really live the beautiful lives we think they do? Is a pretty setting proof of a lovely life?

Is the view of your own life as good from the inside out as it might appear from the outside in? There are folks with amazingly rich and blessed spirits who have no outward trappings of privilege. Which is most important?

The more we begin to recognize the truths of relationship, the more our vision sharpens. Abandonment has many faces, like the starving children in a TV commercial or a lonely suburban wife whose husband and family are far too busy to see her true needs.

Relationship Required

There are few sights as sad as a horse alone in a pasture or a solitary dog in a yard. Horses are born looking for a herd and dogs are born looking for a pack. For a horse or dog to live apart from relationship is similar to a human living apart from God.

God created both horses and dogs to find security, structure, companionship, and mates in the midst of either a herd or pack. Neither the dog nor horse has a spirit that thrives in solitude. Are humans really so different?

Humans are born looking for God. Horses were created to live in a herd, subject to the laws of their Creator. Humans were created to live in fellowship with each other, craving and being subject to the love and leadership of our Creator. Fellowship with others is necessary to fully inflate our spirits. Most important of all to the health of our spirit is the relationship, or lack thereof, that each of us has with Jesus Christ.

This small, neighboring group of horses has the blessing of herdship. While there is much more possible, they can at least live out their lives with contentment. At the end of each horse's life, its spirit will go to whatever place God selects. No eternal opportunity will have been missed.

The same is not true for people. Sure, there are lots of folks who enjoy plenty of fellowship. Many have large families who are fully engaged in each other's lives, but if they live without a relationship with Jesus Christ they will always know there is *something else*.

[131]

To the casual observer, it may appear that such people live out their lives in contentment. Christians know there is more available and where to find it, just as there is more possible for the small herd of horses the lady from church watches each day.

The difference between the two scenarios is in the eternal opportunity. Not only is the bounty of relationship with Christ missing from the daily walk of these earthbound folks, but where will their spirit go when they pass from this life?

God created the horse for herdship. As long as man doesn't interfere, horses may live as they were meant to. Humans were created to be in relationship with God, not just "herdship" with one another. What is the eternal opportunity that is lost when there is no relationship with Jesus Christ?

There will be no mansion in heaven. There will be no address on file. Wherever that place may be, each horse will eventually reach its eternal home. A horse forced to live alone is a tragedy, but they are never abandoned by their Creator. He knows the whereabouts of every sparrow and every horse. God won't let even one fall through the cracks.

The person who lives without God will not be as fortunate as the simple horse or sparrow. When the life of the human who lived apart from God ends, all possibility for care and provision by his Creator will be lost...forever. Nothing is as tragic as a person apart from God, no matter how extravagant his worldly surroundings.

Praise the Lord we know the good news of the Gospel of Jesus Christ. For each of His children, a home awaits and there is an address on file. There is a mansion prepared especially for you and for me. God never walks away from one of His own. When separation occurs, it is by our choice and action, not His.

Is He Looking for You?

Regardless of the circumstances of your life at this moment, God is busy behind the scenes preparing for your return trip home. He knows where you were yesterday, where you are now, and where to find you tomorrow. God knows your eternal address. When the time is ripe, nothing will prevent you from walking through the open gate to occupy the mansion He prepared especially for you.

If you feel like you're still far, far away from God, perhaps you can speed up the process of getting found by setting out to meet Him along the road that presently separates you. Ask someone near you to help you find the path.

We all need herdship with our fellow man, but more than that, we need a relationship with Jesus Christ.

He Came Looking for Me

LEADERSHIP

The way a halter and lead rope are used speaks volumes about the state of leadership and relationship between human and horse. The ultimate challenge to leadership is to walk away, no halter and no lead rope, and see if the horse will choose to follow anyway. I don't mean follow out of curiosity, but to come when asked and to remain. Even in the earlier stages of relationship, leadership seldom takes the slack out of a lead rope; no pressure is applied. The horse learns to follow, not to be pulled along.

Shiner and Ace have good leading skills with a halter and rope. Shiner is beginning to learn that I don't make promises to him I can't keep, and he chooses to come to me more easily. Ace is doing well, but not as consistently as his brother. The reactive side of Ace's brain is still very much in evidence even though he is a delightful pet most of the time.

"Our Lord never insists upon obedience; He tells us very emphatically what we ought to do, but He never takes means to make us do it."

"He will not help me to obey Him, I must obey Him, and when I do obey Him, I fulfill my spiritual destiny." -- Oswald Chambers

The issue of obedience is important whether we are talking about God, horses, or any other leader/follower relationship. The relationships you have with your children are no exception to the rule. As a horse trainer, I never set out to make a horse obey. My goal is to create a foundation that would give us the means to build relationship and success; to build faith.

Every horse must be free to obey, resist, or simply try to ignore my requests. Obedience does not exist unless the opportunity to *not* obey is present. These are the same three options a Christian has when the Spirit offers training to him or her.

A staple of every program or clinic I present is sharing with my audience the only two reasons why a person or horse will not do as we ask. The only two reasons we do not get obedience from another is that he is either *unable* to obey or *unwilling* to obey.

If unable to obey, we must offer more education or assistance so our student becomes able. Punishment never fixes inability and education never fixes unwillingness. As a horse trainer, it is my job to determine if a horse is unable to perform correctly or if it just doesn't want to perform correctly. In either case I will take the appropriate action.

The best illustration of this point is the relationship between God and Satan. Satan is well acquainted with God. Will more education or assistance bring Satan to worship God? No. Satan is unwilling. Satan knows the truth, he just doesn't care. He is unrepentant and firmly set in opposition to God's plan.

The Holy Spirit teaches us and makes us able to do as God wills. There is no inability God will not correct if we simply allow Him to. Our bit is only to obey and continue to learn. Membership in the family of God is strictly voluntary, unlike the training of some horses.

When asked why I think horses are so useful for teaching humans how to improve their own walk with Jesus Christ I mention the simple fact the God wants the same three things from me that I want from my horses:

1. Show up.

2. Focus.

3. Offer obedience.

When I encounter horses like Ace that are resistant to the training process, it's my responsibility to determine if he or she is unwilling or unable. Unlike the Holy Spirit, my training methods are not perfect and my messages not always perfectly prepared and delivered. When I am clear, however, I know the horse's resistance comes from unwillingness.

"He who has My commandments and obeys them, it is he who loves Me." -- John 14:21

With a specific goal in mind, I continue to work on the relationship, helping the horse in training to understand—and at times *requiring* their obedience. However, if there comes a time when a horse continues to refuse to offer obedience, our relationship ends. A new horse gets the stall, the opportunity, and the dance begins anew.

When testing the degree to which a horse has accepted its training, the best horse trainers (like the Holy Spirit) always offer an opportunity to not obey. There is usually an escape option provided and an opening that allows for movement. My goal is for the horse to choose to obey, to make a decision not to escape, but instead to choose relationship with me.

The training process Christians undergo is never based on fear. The fear I'm talking about here is not the same

[137]

fear as "fearing the Lord." Fear of the Lord is respect for the God of creation. The type of fear, or terror, I mean here does not teach nor does it make one able. Terror only presents an obstacle to the actual lesson unless the lesson itself is one of domination.

The Holy Spirit never offers a lesson plan where domination is the sole topic of the day. A good horse trainer certainly wouldn't either.

John 14:26 tells us that the Lord Jesus Christ left us the Holy Spirit as our helper. In the next verse we read that Jesus also left us peace. "Not as the world gives do I give to you. Let not your heart be troubled, neither let it be afraid."

"Fear knocked at the door. Faith answered. No one was there." -- Old English Saying

As Shiner and I strengthen the foundation of our relationship, any insecurity or trouble of the heart will disappear as he learns to trust the peace I offer to him. My job is to recognize when he becomes anxious or frustrated and solve his problem. Willing horses fail because we either ask too much or we ask in the wrong way. The answer to every challenge must be the release of pressure and perfect peace. As much as is possible, I will be faithful to deliver all that I promise. Our faith in God is well placed and He is always perfect in delivering on what He promised.

Fear plays no part in our training and walk with the Lord. As we learned in an earlier chapter, while fear can be a tool that prepares us for instruction, pure fear itself is an instrument of the enemy, not our helper, the Holy Spirit. Faith is the product of relationship with Jesus Christ through the work of the Spirit.

Is there any problem we can bring before the Lord that He is not able to both understand and fix? In any moment of anxiety, aggression, or anger, God has already prepared a place of release and peace. It is our work to persevere in the search. Horses learn from the release of pressure. Are we so different? Every time we discover that every challenge is met with ultimate peace, faith grows. Faith is the goad that drives fear from our hearts. Only when faith is weak can fear enter our lives.

Our experience under the Spirit's tutelage is one of conviction, not condemnation. Judgment will come, but for Christians who remain in the school of the Spirit, each day confirms our faith in a most worthy Leader.

"To him who overcomes I will give some of the hidden manna to eat. And I will give him a white stone, and on the stone a new name written which no one knows except him who receives it." -- Revelation 2:17

Maintaining Relationship

"But now, after you have known God, or rather are known by God, how is it that you turn again to the weak and beggarly elements, to which you desire again to be in bondage?" -- Galatians 4:9

Two weeks after Ace and Shiner were added to the barn, sending Swizzle and Asti out for the winter, what had been a well ordered and obedient, little herd was now changed into one less orderly and less secure. Recent bad weather kept me from making much progress in building relationship with Ace and Shiner.

Ace is drawn to the mares on the other side of the cross fence. He has developed a habit of running the fence when Asti and Swizzle get tired of talking to him and wander off to other pursuits. At first, Shiner stayed with him, tagging along as Ace trotted, walked, or frantically galloped along the fence line in his discontent. Strangely enough, when the Appaloosa boys were in the front pasture, it was Shiner who trotted the fence in either excitement or anxiety while cool-as-a-cucumber Ace took no notice at all.

For the past couple of days, my little herd has pretty much ignored me when I call them in to supper intending to tuck them into their cozy stalls. Because Ace is so committed to being upset, the other horses keep an eye on him, wondering just where the problem is. They don't see one. But horses have enjoyed long survival thanks to innate herd instincts that bind them together.

This morning the truth of the situation dawned on me. The reason my herd is less responsive is that I have not properly maintained my existing relationship as leader with Copper and Bo, much less in making progress with the new kids in the barn. We are at a tipping point where Copper and Bo actually consider whether they should come to me or stay with the herd.

I have never had to repeatedly call my horses in at night, or any other time for that matter. I appear; they come. Not at the moment, however. There is obviously a need for intervention. The decision point that needs to be addressed is with Copper and Bo and not with the obvious culprit, Ace. I need to strengthen my ties with Bo and Copper so that regardless of what the others do, they will come to me without conscious consideration. It must be an automatic reflex. Our bond must be stronger than the one they have with their herd.

It seems to me that Shiner may be leaning toward joining Bo and Copper, choosing the barn rather than the fence line that is so attractive to Ace. During the day, he spends more and more time with Bo and Copper and less time hanging with his idiot brother Ace. When I called them in last night, I only got three. Not Ace. I did not pursue him. Baber felt bad that Ace was alone and thought he might go out and get Ace to come in. I said no.

Shiner is always aware of me. He appears to be open to relationship, perhaps even asking if there is more to be had. I am encouraged. But Ace is still a completely unknown quantity.

Well. My work is cut out for me. In order to follow the example set by Jesus Christ and the Holy Spirit, I need to get out there regardless of the weather and do some maintenance with Copper and Bo. I must reinforce my role as leader of the herd, and deliver on my promise that security is always found with me. Only when our relationship is healthy will Bo and Copper keep one eye and one ear tuned to the landscape in case I appear.

Now that I realize the failure is mine, I will somehow make time for Bo and Copper today. It is cold, and I have Reynaud's, a disease that limits the circulation in my hands and feet. That consideration must be put aside. A weakness in foundation has come to light. I would be a poor leader indeed if I ignored the needs of my "followers" simply for my own physical comfort.

Remember the illustration of the burning barn? If I allow the cords of relationship to fray too much with Bo and Copper, they could be exposed to mortal danger if fear overcomes their weakened faith in me. They might not follow me through a burning barn. Religion won't lead you through the flames to freedom, but relationship will. Only by relationship with Jesus Christ are we safe from worldly dangers. No matter how intense the fire, we are safe with Him. Like all relationships, ours with Jesus also needs routine maintenance to remain strong and resilient.

Christians may never rest on their laurels of relationship with God. Busy schedules, illness, and the myriad wealth of distractions in the world lure us away from spending regular time with the Spirit. Only by proximity and by regular time spent together, are we able to maintain a healthy and vibrant relationship with Jesus Christ.

Do you keep an eye and ear tuned to the Spirit? Or are you beginning to drift into a more comfortable relationship with your own herd, building a wall between you and the Lord rather than building upon a strong foundation?

If you recognize that you have been running your own fence line in either anxiety or discontent, stop the wasted motion and focus instead on the Master. Turn around. The Holy Spirit is there waiting for you to come back. He is ever faithful.

Balancing Authority and Humility

One cannot properly be *in* authority without being in equal measure *under* authority. Authority and humility must be balanced against each other to produce one who blesses the relationships they share. On cannot be a great leader if one is unable to be a great follower. Jesus Christ is the perfect illustration of this truth. He is God and He is human. He did only the will of His Father and yet He is also the King of Kings.

After completing a refresher course in leader-follower relations with Bo, I realized just how far off track we had strayed. When I began working in the arena my fearless Bo was more concerned with the two mismatched Australian Shepherds running up and down the backyard fence than with the nuances of my cues and directions.

Normally, Bo wouldn't even notice the hairy little yappers running outside the fence. Today they were a serious distraction to him. How surprising and how humbling. We went back to work on the foundations of our relationship. In less than fifteen minutes Bo returned his focus to me and taught me a hard lesson in the process.

Once Bo and I finished our session playing puzzles, he followed me through the arena gate to the pasture. When I was certain I still had his attention and that he was calm and settled, I took off his halter and dismissed him from class. Bo went out to join Copper, Shiner, and Ace in the pasture behind the barn.

While still bundled up like an Eskimo I figured I might as well clean the barn. As I picked both stalls and pens, I watched the behavior of the boys in the bright sunshine of a winter morning that looks so inviting—if you are indoors looking out. Sunshine yes; below freezing—also yes.

After only a few minutes, I realized one of the casualties of my failure to maintain my relationship with Bo was his confidence in his own leadership ability. Bo is the leader of the herd. Asti controlled the pasture society for a long time, but once Bo and I attained a certain level of relationship, his obedience to my authority translated into his authority as herd leader. Bo challenged Asti and took over responsibility for what then became his herd.

[143]

Even before the Appaloosa boys swapped places with Asti and Swizzle, Bo was the undisputed king and guardian of the pasture. Now that I realize Bo had lost some of his confidence, I see that he was no longer acting as the leader. No other horse stepped into the vacuum left when Bo relinquished his authority to assume responsibility for the herd. Only now did I realize that Bo had abdicated his authority and no longer considered himself the leader and guardian of the herd. Insecurity had been king of the pasture recently.

Bo lost his confidence in both his calling and ability to be responsible for the safety and direction of the herd because he lost the absolute confidence he had in me as *his* leader. I never realized the absence of herd leadership until I saw Bo reclaim it today. Once Bo and I reconnected he was in a totally different state of mind. He was soft. He was confident. He was focused. He was focused on me again.

Order Is Restored

After releasing Bo, I watched Ace begin to trot over to the fence line dividing our place from the neighbor's. The lone paint horse next door is without pasture mates except for the bucking bull breeding stock that graze alongside him. Since the paint's two horse friends moved away recently, the young gelding hugs the fence hoping to find herdship with our horses.

As Ace increased his speed and intent, Shiner saw him and headed off to join his brother. Shiner is caught between Ace and the other two. He doesn't know where his allegiance should be. This is further evidence of an absence of herd leadership. There shouldn't be any question about where Shiner should go; the four horses should behave cohesively as one family unit.

[144]

Horses are hard-wired to follow the leader. When not with me, my horses need to have a healthy order within the herd so this innate need for security and direction is met. The herd leader sets the tone for all herd responses. When the leader is calm, the herd is calm. When the leader calls for retreat, get out of the way because there will be a stampede. The leader ensures the safety of the herd when they put their heads down to drink or eat, behaviors that in the wild would leave them momentarily vulnerable to predators.

Once Shiner left Bo and Copper's company, a change came upon the pasture. Bo realized that Shiner was leaving him and going to Ace. Bo made a decision, though I doubt he made it consciously. Bo took off at a fast trot, then accelerated to a lope in the direction Shiner and Ace were heading. Sensing that something important was about to happen, Copper followed behind Bo at a brisk lope. Copper usually ignores the others when they run around for no particular reason. Even laid back Copper somehow knew this was different.

I continued to observe this interesting development as I sorted frozen apples from the dirt and shavings of each horse's pen. You can learn a lot from watching horses.

Bo quickly reached Ace and Shiner, who had just arrived at the place on the fence where the paint waited, eagerly jogging up and down a short section of fence line hoping to lure our horses over to him. Without stopping to check out the particulars, Bo rounded up Ace and Shiner and started herding them away from the fence. Copper arrived and Bo sent them all away, driving them with purpose and authority.

Ace tried to circle back and return to the fence to resume his visit with the paint. Bo emphatically said no.

[145]

In the horse world, the leader is the one who controls the feet of the other. If I control the horse's feet, I am the leader. In the case of horse and horse, the concept remains the same. Bo took back control of the other dozen horse feet in the pasture. Bo reestablished his authority. Ace, Shiner, and Copper went where Bo sent them, and at the speed Bo commanded.

This is when it dawned on me that I had not seen any evidence of authority from Bo since we made the change in herd composition. It just so happened that we adopted a stray miniature Aussie on almost the same day we put Swizzle and Asti out and brought Ace and Shiner in to the barn. That fact alone caused a significant disruption in the normal order of the place, to be sure.

Squeak is fast and can be difficult to ignore at times. When this event combined with bad weather and the lack of my involvement with Bo, the result was his abdication of authority. With his security at low tide in our relationship, he had no longer been confident enough to provide herd leadership.

The Leadership Chain

Just the short time Bo and I spent today working on the foundation of our relationship gave Bo enough confidence to resume the leadership role again in his herd. It was my failure to sufficiently maintain my authority over Bo that caused him to abdicate his place as herd leader. It was the reinforcement of our relationship as leader and follower that allowed Bo to restore his authority over the herd.

There is little in life that is truly compartmentalized from all else. We deceive ourselves when we think otherwise. The connection between authority and humility is

[146]

made on the basis of security and position. Great leaders must also be great followers. Poor followers seldom make good leaders.

God is at the absolute top of the leadership chain. He reports to no one. There is no one on earth in a position of authority who will not ultimately report to God.

Much of the failure of society today is due to the lack of balance between authority and humility. Fathers cannot properly lead their families if they are not likewise under the proper authority of God.

Soldiers begin to learn the absolute requirement of balanced leader/follower relationships the moment they walk through the gate into boot camp. No one who serves in uniform is the top of the leadership chain, at least not in the United States. As the new recruit masters the skills required for proper followership, he or she begins to climb the ladder of authority.

How can a father make a critical decision for his family if he has no security in relationship with the Lord? There is no strength to draw upon.

How can a major make a life and death decision involving his or her soldiers if the general waffles at every turn?

Failing to maintain strong relationship with our children puts them at risk. Only by remaining secure in their relationship with you will your child be able to lead others effectively and confidently. Children without confidence in the relationship they have with their parents cannot perform well in a leadership role with peers. A boy or girl who leads a club or sporting team must remain under proper authority in order to serve those who look to them for direction or guidance. When any link in the leadership chain is compromised, eventually all will be.

When we fail as Christians to live by the example we preach, we are not only failing in our relationship with God, but we may be negatively impacting someone else's walk.

No man is an island. It is nearly impossible to exist when completely independent of others. We may ultimately walk alone with the Lord, but He uses us in places of authority to keep those within our herd working together in security and unity. We will only succeed in our roles of both leader and follower if we remain in proper relationship with Him.

Insecurity became the ruler of the pasture when the horses were separated from relationship with me. My fault. The king of this world now controls the earth. Insecurity rules society because the leadership is no longer under the proper authority of God.

*"I will no longer talk much with you, for
the ruler of this world is coming, and he has nothing in
Me."- John 14:30*

When I failed through neglect to be in proper authority over Bo the entire herd suffered. That has now been corrected. And while I dropped the ball, you may be certain that your spiritual Leader will never fail you.

Do the leaders you recognize in your life balance their authority with equal humility as followers of a higher leader? Do you?

TEMPTATION

Have you ever had a dream or vision that you know came directly from the Lord? What was it? Did it make you fearful? Did you overcome a challenge?

Recently I had a dream about carrying a message God gave me. I wasn't brilliantly clever in the scenario of dream; I was a writer. Just a week earlier I had a similar dream. This latest experience was quite different.

In the first dream, I awoke victorious from the challenge presented. Even while asleep, I recognized that the Enemy was trying to get me to play the part he had written for me in the drama. I recognized it for what it was and shut the dream down even though I continued to sleep. When I woke, I prayed a prayer of thanksgiving that I had both recognized the temptation and rejected it. *This*, I thought, *is a reward of relationship.*

Sometimes we accept victory a little too eagerly. It can be a mistake to rest too quickly on our laurels, as my experience with Bo recently proved. Circumstances change much too quickly to stop being ever vigilant. Overcoming is a work of every day, not something a human will ever master.

The day after the second dream was Sunday. That morning, when I brought the horses in before leaving for church, each entered his gate as usual; politely and in the proper order. Once in his house, however, Shiner became fixated on something south of the barn that I could neither see nor hear. Perhaps it was the paint horse on the next place or something only Shiner was aware of in his own special world.

Once I realized that Shiner was not his newly calm and contented self, I walked through his stall and out into his pen to ask him to redirect his attention away from whatever was causing him concern and back on to me. He obviously had a problem and it was my job to fix it - imagined or not.

Life sometimes happens in fits and starts whether in real life or in the narrative of a book. I'll get back to the dream but first Shiner needs to be addressed.

There should never be a reason for one of my horses to be upset, anxious, or nervously focused on anything. I try to be faithful to recognize the times when any insecurity appears, take steps to resolve any issue, and return the horse to a state of grace, if you will. Peace, joy, and grace; the heart of the barn and the heart of the home.

As a leader worthy of my horse's trust, I must be faithful to step in whenever I see that one of them is momentarily vulnerable to temptations of distraction. No matter what else is on the list for the day, everything stops when it appears the security of being in right relationship with me is disturbed (or, as was the case with Bo, when I finally noticed that our relationship was disturbed.)

The morning after the second dream was no exception. I set aside routine and engaged Shiner in a simple foundational relationship exercise. It seemed to work exactly as I had hoped and planned.

Just before I left Shiner's stall, I went to give him one more pat, a reinforcement of the bond that focused his attention on to me and returned him to a balanced and contented state. Shiner eats with the off side of his body up against the front wall of his stall. The feeder is in the corner, so I had to walk by his hip to get to the stall door. Before leaving I just wanted to have him step over and away with his hindquarters so I could stroke his neck and withers in a final farewell before heading back to the house.

The first request I make to a horse to move his feet is made with body language. That presumes, of course, that I have its attention and it takes note of my movement, however slight. Shiner either didn't notice or failed to pay attention—I don't know which, and it doesn't matter—the result is the same.

My suggestion for Shiner to move wasn't heeded, so I then made a specific request by using a clicking sound. That clicking sound is the universal cue I use to request movement. The situation and my body position serve as indicators of *what* I want moved; the click just means "move."

I clicked; again no response. Shiner just kept busy with his breakfast. He didn't care that I was at his hip. Shiner came to us with a tendency to kick whenever something or someone came near while he was eating, but we took care of that a long time ago. I wasn't concerned about being kicked or pinned between his body and the front of the stall, but being ignored raised a big, red relationship flag all its own.

While the big, white hip in front of me caused no concern for my safety, I was, however, a bit surprised when neither my suggestion nor my direct request had resulted in the movement I expected Shiner to make. Again, as a leader

[151]

worthy of trust, I was required to take action. I left Shiner's stall, walked across the breezeway and into the tack room. With halter and lead rope in hand, I returned to Shiner's stall.

The Gamble of Giving a Direct Order

One of the secrets of great horsemen, remarkable parents, and exceptional leaders in general is knowing when to give an order and when not to. We take a serious gamble whenever we give a horse, a child, or a subordinate a direct order. Should they choose to refuse, we find ourselves face-to-face with a dicey situation.

Great leaders never give a direct order unless they have a near certainty that the one receiving the order will either obey immediately—or the leader is nearly certain he or she can *require* obedience. Giving an order and just hoping that it will be followed is the habit of one who doesn't understand the responsibility that is married to the authority of leadership.

Once I had my tools in hand, I walked purposefully into Shiner's stall, went to his near side (where I had lots of room behind me...) and asked Shiner to move away from his feeder. I knew I could require movement and so did he. Shiner backed a step or two and looked at me.

In a completely nonchalant manner, I fastened the rope halter on Shiner's head. My next move was to suggest he move his hindquarters in a similar manner to the suggestion he had ignored a minute earlier. Shiner didn't snap around as he should, although he gave me "lip service" and kind of wallowed his butt away from me.

Leaders give precise cues and expect precise responses. We do not accept half-hearted attempts to placate us.

[152]

The end of my lead rope engaged Shiner's hip firmly but without any emotion. It was nothing more than a specific cue to remind him how the foundational exercise worked. That big, beautiful hip smartly yielded and Shiner's attention was rooted to me.

The lesson continued as it always did: yield the hindquarters from one side, then the other. Back away with a simple hand gesture; approach again with a small postural invitation. In the span of ninety seconds, Shiner was obedient, focused, content, and perfectly happy to stand, head lowered and eyes soft, enjoying the small scratches my fingers made on the cowlick between his eyes. All thoughts of breakfast were forgotten and we shared a wonderful moment.

Shiner's halter was removed and I suggested he yield his body—he responded perfectly. When I left his stall, he watched me until I was nearly to the tack room door before he remembered breakfast and turned to his feeder.

So, What about That Dream?

Okay, so now we can go back to where we started at the beginning of this story, the second dream. You will remember that this dream was similar to one I had a week earlier. During that first dream I recognized the temptation to be distracted and was immediately obedient and focused on the author of my dreams. The result was sweet victory.

My second nocturnal performance wasn't quite as snappy. All horse owners and parents know that one of their "children" performing a lesson correctly one time in no way guarantees a correct response each and every time that same challenge arises.

Amazing Grays the book, and Amazing Grays the ministry, both celebrated an official beginning the week I had the second dream. My husband and I were now officially messengers for the Lord. The book was released by the publisher and we celebrated the launch of both book and ministry at a public event here in Parker County.

In addition to the launch event, we attended and made short presentations at a number of other public events. Our job is to correctly and faithfully carry a message of grace and victory in Jesus Christ to the family of God. This is a very new and very different job for both of us.

In my latest dream, I was trying to share God's message with people who insisted on taking the conversation in a completely different direction. The atmosphere of the gathering was tough. There were a lot of unhappy and fearful people there, all vying for a chance to tell the others just how bad things were for them.

As I sat with the second or third group of people, I realized I had to move on to greener pastures and quit casting pearls before the group of totally uninterested "swine" (no disrespect intended, that's just how the verse reads.) I told the folks around the table that I needed to get back to my job. One of the people at the table got up when I did and asked to speak with me privately. *Wow, this might be a good opportunity to share.* Expectantly, I agreed.

Sometimes I am asked to have a personal conversation with someone when my message has hit home or when it is not completely understood, but is at least being given serious consideration by the listener. In a way, it's like the untrained horse in the round pen starting to follow the human around just a bit. There is no commitment yet—but there is at least the potential for focus and consideration.

The person referred back to the message I had been trying to share and basically asked why I thought I was qualified to offer my opinion. What they really wanted to know was whether I had any street cred. Did I have the personal experience that made my words worth listening to? In response, I started itemizing the experiences I had that directly pertained to overcoming personal difficulties and my life experiences that rivaled those presently causing such angst around the tables—and for this person in particular.

Where did I go wrong?

Once I had shared my specific and relevant experience, I paused and then just had to add one more little tidbit that had absolutely nothing to do with the matter at hand. What I added was, "And by the way, I had a book launched this week that sold out at Amazon." I had departed from sharing useful information and sank to the level of trying to make myself sound important. *How quickly I got up to my knees in the quick sand ...*

The person in the dream appeared to be growing ever more impressed with my credentials of life experience, so I played right into that temptation and tried to grab hold of just a bit more. *In the twinkling of an eye the quick sand was around my chest...*

When I put my first foot through the door of temptation by going off-message, that nasty little door of opportunity opened even wider, warmly inviting me to put the second foot through. The person in my dream told me he was heavily involved in casting a movie and wanted me to be in it. After all, I was so unique, so wonderful. (Do you see where this is going?) I agreed and even suggested my husband be included.

The dream ended. I failed. *And I disappeared under the quick sand altogether...*

Failure Usually Comes by Way of Our Strengths

When I woke up, I realized what had happened. I had failed to stay focused on message, on relationship, and had succumbed to carnal desire—much like Shiner did yesterday morning. Was it any coincidence that I had the dream that night and not a week later? I think not.

Shiner was comforted and returned to a place of security and balance by my presence in his stall. He responded to me and found safety in our relationship—until the food distracted him. Then I lost his attention even though he didn't ignore me on purpose.

In my first dream, I stayed clearly focused on message and on the Lord. I overcame temptation by recognizing it as soon as it appeared and rejected it. I was victorious.

In that second dream I was doing a great job of sharing His message—until the powerful distractions of pride and personality showed up. Is this what being a new author is like? Get a book published and fall flat on your face? Boy did I fall. I stepped right into it with a loud squish.

Temptation usually finds a way to get to us on the battlefield where we are the most confident in our abilities, not through the swirling mists of doubt we feel lurking behind us that keep our antennae most sharply tuned. It's much more difficult for temptation to wiggle through on a flank we keep heavily guarded because we recognize our shortcomings.

I am confident in the message we've been given. I am confident in *Amazing Grays,* the book. But in my dream, it didn't take much to strike me down right in the very place where I was most confident. Claiming any personal right to the message was my downfall. The message isn't unique to me or my husband. The message has been around for two thousand years.

The good news is that God is forever faithful to step in—every time—and take steps to redirect our feet, to return us to a state of grace, even if it means a firm slap on our hip with His lead rope. I am thankful my ego got a good and deserved bruising. Like Shiner, it put me back into a place of peace and security. And also like Shiner, I'm sure I'll be visiting that place of correction again.

HE CAME LOOKING FOR ME

NEVER TOO LATE

"These last worked only one hour and you made them equal to us who have borne the burden and the heat of the day."

-- Matthew 20:12

In the parable of the vineyard owner all workers received the same reward; one denarius. Some had worked the entire day, others just one hour. When wages were paid, the workers who had been in the field the longest expected a bonus. When they saw that those who entered in to the vineyard to work for only a short while received a full day's wage they vigorously objected.

The point of this parable is that it is never too late. The ultimate reward of relationship with Jesus Christ will be fully as sweet for those who come to Him later as for those who walked faithfully with Him their entire lives.

What about the person who chooses to put the question of relationship with Christ in the 'to do later' box, counting on converting just in time to claim a full reward? You might remind them that even the vineyard workers who came late accepted the offer of employment as soon as it was made. They didn't flake away the day and run looking for work at the last hour.

A decision delayed may become a decision denied. There is no parable in the Bible where Jesus tells someone to

[159]

follow Him whenever it seems more convenient. Every offer He made was accepted or rejected at the time. The rich young ruler who basically told Jesus he would "get back to Him" once he'd taken care of business did not get a second chance. When Jesus says *"Come to Me,"* you must answer yes or no; "Check with me later" isn't an option.

Is there any difference in the relationship I have with my horses based upon the length of time we have lived together? Is my bond stronger with Swizzle, the only horse that has spent its entire life with us? I have logged more saddle hours with Asti than with any of my other horses. Should that make her higher on my relationship scale than Bo or Shiner?

Do you have an order of preference of your children? Sure, each of your parent-child relationships is different from the others. But, is one more important than the others? And if so, why? Everyone probably agrees that parents should not prefer one child over another. In a perfect world that would certainly be the case, but we don't live in a perfect world.

If you have one child who has refused your every attempt to build a strong relationship with him, it is only reasonable to be less bonded to him. God knows when we refuse relationship with Him. Such refusals matter.

One day I rode Shiner after an entire day on the tractor mowing pastures. I had promised myself that I would saddle and ride *somebody*. The commitments of launching *Amazing Grays* had kept us busy for over a month and the unusually wet weather of both winter and early spring had made riding a near impossibility.

Mowing pastures is wonderful therapy for me. I find it rewarding in a number of ways. First, it provides instant gratification. Our flail mower leaves a neat, even carpet of green behind it as my tractor works its way down the field. While I am one who appreciates the instant gratification of both mowing grass and painting walls, there is also a blessing of service found in mowing, though not so much for painting. My horses are provided with a clean plate, heaped with nutritious food, and I am able to be a good steward of what the Lord has provided for our use.

What I appreciate more than anything else is the time I spend alone with the Lord when tracing neat rows up one side of the pasture and down the other. There is nothing between us, no disturbances or distractions to interfere with our conversation. One of the great things about mowing for me is that I tend to spend way more time listening during these conversations than I do sharing my own opinions and ideas.

Have you noticed that we don't learn a whole lot by listening to ourselves talk? Mowing usually keeps my mouth from moving and my ears engaged. The wonderful therapy of mowing brought me back to my proper place, focusing on my Master and not on my to-do list.

My ride on Shiner was pretty good. I turned the other horses out into the pasture when I began grooming him. He had not been saddled for at least a couple of weeks. At first, his attention seemed to follow his pasture mates right back out to the freshly cut grass. Still, it didn't seem to be too big a deal to get him to refocus on the matter at hand and I prepared to mount up.

Well, he did offer one little, extra "comment." I saddled him without any particular issue. We walked to the arena to longe just for a minute as one last, little check on Shiner's concentration before I climbed into the saddle. The other horses tend to stay as close to me as possible and were their normal, little inquisitive selves. All three hung pretty close to the arena fence as I led Shiner into the arena to entertain my equine audience.

Any of the other three would have been happy to have been chosen for attention today. Even though Shiner was the winner, the others were determined to participate in any way possible. So of course Shiner's full attention wasn't on me. I asked Shiner to start off in a counter-clockwise circle by pointing the way and I fully expected him to immediately start moving his feet. He almost always complied obediently. There is a distinct difference between *always* and *almost always*. Today was apparently not Shiner's day for reflexive obedience.

Shiner took about three bumpy strides, put his head down, humped a few more strides, then quit and turned to face me. No words were exchanged, and his feet didn't move again, but his communication was perfect.

"Do you think you can make me?"

Shiner very clearly was challenging my authority. This was something new from Shiner. He had been distracted in the past, insecure in the past, even a tad resistant—but had never directly confronted me this way.

No matter. My answer was an immediate, "I don't think I can, young man - I know I can." Shiner wasn't mad at me. Shiner probably didn't even think really hard about what he was doing. He just knew he wasn't with the other horses and wanted to let me know he had a different idea about how his afternoon should be spent.

Five minutes later, Shiner and I returned to the exact spot where his pretence of obedience had ended. This time

[162]

he set out like a perfect gentleman when I asked him to navigate a counter-clockwise circle around me. My leadership pedestal was back to its proper height and the riding portion of our time together began.

Have you ever found yourself challenging God? You know you have received direction on what or how to do a task, yet you stiffen and say, "Do you think you can make me?" Many times we challenge God in just this way and aren't even consciously aware that we did it. We aren't mad at God. We didn't even give our response much thought. We just knew we had other plans...

Shiner didn't confuse me by his challenge, and I assure you, God is not confused either.

Results of Rebellion

When we rebel, our level of peace, joy, and security diminishes because we have removed God from His throne. Not in actuality of course, but the result of this ebbing of faith from its proper level leaves us mistakenly believing we have more authority and power than we truly possess.

When you find yourself stiffening or bristling as you read the Word or hear His message, stop immediately and consider the issue. What is causing such a response, such rebellion? And yes, it is rebellion. Whenever we get our back up when reading the Bible, it is a brilliant flare signaling our failure to acknowledge God's authority over us in some way.

Why are you challenging Him on this point? What is so important to you that you are willing to look God square in the face and ask, "Do you think you can?" There will never be a time when God's answer to your challenge will be anything other than, "Yes, I *can*."

[163]

When I contemplated the results of my day on the tractor and experience with Shiner, I came to this conclusion: I can't do everything. What needs to be done is what God asks me to do. Sure, there are the basics of caring for family, home, property, and animals. Okay, the animals are family, too. I expect you know what I meant.

As a horse trainer, I always tried to bring each horse along until its highest and best use was established. If it was as a jumper, we pursued that foundation and I sent them off to be a jumper. When the horse's greatest talent was consistency and even-temper, it was directed toward some event that required great precision or riders who need unusually steady mounts.

Horses can be well broke and/or highly trained. My trainer boots want me to attain these goals with every horse; well broke *and* highly trained. The two are not necessarily the same. A horse may be well broke but have little higher education. Other horses have the equivalent of an Equine PhD, but are not well broke.

What I learned yesterday is that I need only bring Swizzle, Shiner, and Ace into the camp of the well broke, that is, into right relationship with me. It is doubtful they will ever perform for a third-party judge. The only opinion that matters is mine. Being in right relationship to me will allow them to get along well with everyone else as well, whether equine or human.

The workers hired by the vineyard owner early in the day are like Asti and Bo. Each entered training early and learned much more than the ones who came into the barn later. Asti may always be the most highly trained horse we own, even though she isn't in the barn all that often anymore.

Shiner, on the other hand, is starting his training as a seriously middle-aged horse, well into the afternoon of the working day. And Ace? Ace will be offered employment at an even later hour and I'll have to wait to see whether or not he accepts it.

Shiner not only accepted my offer, he accepted it with enthusiasm. There is a learning curve to work through, but I have no doubt he will eventually be a happy balanced horse and enjoy his new position in our family.

"Whether one traces his Americanism back three centuries to the Mayflower, or three years to the steerage, is not half so important as whether his Americanism of today is real and genuine. No matter by what various crafts we came here, we are all now in the same boat." -- Calvin Coolidge

Each of our horses was offered and accepted employment at different hours of the day. Most will become well-broke, being part of a rewarding family relationship with Baber, with me, and with one another. The amount of the reward will have nothing to do with when they started working. Just like the workers hired to the vineyard, each will receive the same blessing.

Christianity Has No Scorecard

As children of God, we aren't graded on any scale other than the quality of our relationship with Jesus Christ. It doesn't matter if we came into the relationship as babes or seniors. Some of us got there early and have been in training, working in the vineyard for years. Our reward will be the same as those hired at the end of the day—a mansion in Heaven.

The only question that matters in this instance is, "When the offer of employment was made, did you accept?"

Have you been asked the question? If not, let me ask it here. Do you accept? The degree of training we receive is unimportant. There is no third-party judge whose opinion matters in the slightest. The only One we need focus on is Jesus Christ.

Relationships are not based upon any skill set; they are based upon trust, affiliation, security, and love. Swizzle and Shiner will be well-broke and I will love them. Asti and Bo will always have more education than the others and we will love them as well. There is no difference in their standing in the family. They will be loved as long as they live.

God does not respect personal status, wealth, power, or earthly privilege. Works are the natural result of faith. There is no hierarchy of value among the member of Christ's flock based on what we do, but who we are in relationship to Him. Whatever your highest and best use is on earth, all that truly matters is relationship. Learn your lessons well, accept employment when it is offered, and cherish the relationship it brings.

Shiner and Ace were separated from us for years. And yet here they are, home again—for good. We went looking for them. We found them.

"The sheep hear His voice; and He calls His sheep by name and leads them out." -- John 10:3

PRICELESS

Anna Sewell's book, *Black Beauty*, was the first book written that developed the message of relationship shared between horse and human in a way that touched hundreds of thousands, if not millions, of people. The message it contains is powerful enough that most who read it remember it. I sure did.

Black Beauty is thought by many to have been written in 1877 as a children's tale. It was not. Ms. Sewell wrote it to educate those who worked with horses, to try and improve the lives of the cart and dock horses of the nineteenth century. I read it as a young girl and was forever changed. Recently I read it again. If you have a love of all things equine, I highly recommend it to you.

Nearly one hundred thirty-five years later, *Black Beauty* is still on point and this first-person horse narrative is just as fresh and revealing of the equine spirit and the emotions of those who love them today as it was so many years ago. As a testament to the book's place in human-horse societal evolution, the first edition inscribed by Anna Sewell to her mother sold at auction in 2006 for thirty-three thousand pounds sterling, or the equivalent of approximately forty thousand dollars.

In Ms. Sewell's tale, Black Beauty's idyllic formative years end when Squire Gordon's estate is dispersed due to family illness. Beauty is sold to another household where the squire honestly believed he would live out his life and be dealt with honestly and fairly. Sadly, it was not to be.

Beauty's friend, an older pony named Merrylegs, had already earned the highest status a horse can attain in any family when the squire was forced to disperse his property and animals. Unlike Black Beauty, Merrylegs was *never to be sold*. The squire gave Merrylegs to the vicar's family as a trusted mount for his children along with the strict stipulation that he would never be sold. Further, the vicar agreed that when Merrylegs arrived at the end of his useful life, he would be shot and buried.

At first, the word "shot" is jarring to the horse lover's soul. But upon reflection, this blessing bestowed upon Merrylegs was without equal. He would never be sold. The final chapter of Merrylegs's life was written even before his master knew he would need to liquidate his estate and move to a different climate with his sick wife.

Through relationship, Merrylegs became a chosen spirit, adopted into the squire's family and never to be sent off to fend for himself, alone in the world. Unfortunately, as beloved as Black Beauty was to this family, he did not enjoy the same blessing.

Never to Be Sold

There is no higher honor for any horse than that of *never to be sold*. The details of earthly life are uncertain, and wise parents make arrangements for the care of their children in the event of untimely death. Horse owners also need to make arrangements for the care of their horses in case of personal catastrophe.

[168]

You are responsible to make arrangements for any living creature under your ownership or protection. The type of arrangements you make depend upon the relationship you have with each of those creatures. Has your horse attained family status? Are you committed to the relationship until death do you part? You are certainly not a bad person if you answered no to the previous question. However, if you answered yes, then you can begin to appreciate the blessing we receive as the chosen of God.

General Silver

One horse who left a set of very deep hoof prints on my heart is General Silver. General was one of my most influential instructors as I learned to become a horse trainer. In addition to being one of the most opinionated horses I ever dealt with, he also became my very first show horse.

General Siiver

The time came in my career when General no longer had a regular job. We were promoting horses from our own breeding program and my stalls were full of other horses to train. While I didn't show General anymore, he continued to regularly work for a couple of years as a pony horse for our weanlings and yearlings. Eventually we began to use a golf cart to pony, which left General without any job at all.

Given the status General had in my heart, I knew I would never put him up for sale. However, one day a lady came by to look at another horse. She seemed to offer the perfect home for General, so I introduced them to each other. She bought General and took him out of the area to live in the mountains as her best friend. I knew I could never see General as someone else's horse, so sending him far away worked for me.

Please take note that not putting a horse up for sale is obviously not the same as *never to be sold*. Squire Gordon sold Black Beauty to what he hoped would be the perfect home. I did the same with General. We were both wrong, but for different reasons.

Circumstances change. Black Beauty should have had a wonderful life with the squire and his family. He did, until catastrophic illness in the family changed everything. General would have had a wonderful life with his new owner, but like the squire's family, the lady's husband died unexpectedly, leaving her devastated.

I had no idea that all this had happened. We received Christmas cards for a number of years telling us how wonderful and beloved General was. Eventually the cards stopped coming, but I thought nothing of it.

[170]

One day, seven years after General left in someone else's trailer, he came home again in mine. One of my customers wanted me to look at a horse she fancied at a horse trader's barn in the area. I was not enthusiastic about anything this trader might offer, but as her trainer I was obligated to at least go look with her.

It was winter in Arizona. The weather was beautiful, a sky so clear and crisp it might have been fine crystal. It was cold, so we waited to go to the trader's place till around nine that morning. I'll skip all the detail except to tell you that I found General in that trader's barn.

By noon, General was safely home, bundled into a clean blanket, munching alfalfa in a stall deeply bedded in fresh shavings. I learned the difference that day between "not offered for sale" and "never to be sold."

The best plans of man often fail. Once a horse leaves us, we lose all control over its future. General became a horse who would never be sold. I don't know all that happened to him in the years between the home I sent him to and his return to ours. He came home with issues that let me know all had not been perfect. Shiner is a repeat of that experience in some ways.

General moved with us to Texas. We worked on getting him back into the show pen, but he was no longer 100 percent sound. But I rode him some, loved him a lot, and he not only decorated our front pasture, but was the perfect guardian for all our newly weaned foals.

General was my beloved friend until he passed on to even greener pastures. General continued to both bless and teach me until the day he died.

He Came Looking for Me
He Came Looking for Me

The Spotted Wonder

If you read *Amazing Grays, Amazing Grace* you've already met The Spotted Wonder, Abduls Bright Sky. Those of you who haven't read that book know from this one that Sky is Ace and Shiner's sire.

I won't repeat too much of his story except to say that Sky was one who was *never to be sold.* I was there when he took his first breath and also there when his noble chest settled for the last time and his heart stilled.

Once during Sky's successful show career he was up in Flagstaff, Arizona at a National Reining Horse Association competition. The trainer who was riding him called to tell us that the "Italians" wanted to buy Sky and take him to Italy. Without a thought or asking even one question, I said no.

This is probably not the usual response one gets from owners when a lucrative offer hits the table for a horse. Our trainer replied, "But, you don't know how much money they've offered. It's a huge amount." Again without thinking, I said, "There isn't enough money in Italy to buy Sky."

Sky was never to be sold.

Like General, later in his life Sky was also without a real job and spent a lot of time in the pasture with his small herd. Sky was an amazingly talented horse, though not without his idiosyncrasies—nearly all of which were caused by humans.

I called a wonderful trainer who had known Sky for most of his life and always admired him. Not wanting Sky to simply become an old pasture horse, I asked if he had any need for Sky and his talents. He did, and Sky spent the next year in that trainer's barn. It was understood that when his temporary job assignment ended, Sky would return home to me.

After a year, I got a call saying that Sky was getting nervous at shows and becoming more difficult for the non-pro showing him to handle. Sky was at home with me the next day. Within a week, I knew why he was nervous; he was going blind.

Sky's story is a long and complex one, full of lessons, victories, and failures. I assure you, all the failures were mine. *Amazing Grays* ends with a chapter devoted to Sky and our story together. The point that matters here is that Sky was never to be sold. At least in that, I was always faithful to him.

God made provision for us even before we knew we would need it. Being but a simple horse, Merrylegs did not comprehend the benefit he received as a horse adopted into his human family. Through relationship, Merrylegs was fortunate to gain "never to be sold" protection.

Christians are hard pressed to comprehend the blessing we have received as children either born to or adopted into the family of God. No matter our circumstance, no matter the events of the world, we will never be removed from our secure and permanent home with the Lord. We will never be sold.

Squire Gordon did not randomly choose just any of his horses to go to the vicarage; he chose Merrylegs. Baber and I did not go out to find just any Appaloosa, or just any one of Sky's offspring. We went looking for Shiner and Ace. We found them.

Like their father before them, my Appaloosa boys will never be sold. To finish that thought, none of our horses will ever be sold. Not Bo, Swizzle, Copper, Asti, Shiner, or Ace. Should circumstances arise that prevent us from managing the day-to-day care of any of our horses, we will be faithful to make arrangements just as the Squire did for Merrylegs.

"Just as He chose us in Him before the foundation of the world, that we should be holy and without blame before Him in love, having predestined us to adoption as sons by Jesus Christ Himself, according to the good pleasure of His will."
-- Ephesians 1:3-4

"And you also will bear witness, because you have been with Me from the beginning." -- John 15:27

As a child of God, your future is certain. Jesus has already prepared a mansion with your name on the gate post. There will be no substitutions, and no other person will be allowed entrance into the eternal home prepared just for you. God loses none.

Even if you feel lost today, as Shiner and Ace did, you are no more alone than they were. Plans have been made to bring you home. God knows where you are, what your circumstances are, and your path will intersect with the road that leads to the narrow gate just when you are most in need of being found.

By His amazing grace, our home pasture awaits and the gate is open to welcome us in. He promised.

FOCUS ON TODAY

One frequently assumes that beginnings and ends are the most noteworthy or valuable moments. Not necessarily so. In fact, seldom is the first or last of anything the most significant, except perhaps to an antiques dealer.

Live each day as if it were your last. One day it will be.

The book of Malachi speaks of an in-between period in biblical history, the time between the Old Testament and the coming of the Messiah, Jesus Christ. The books of the Old Testament educate, record, admonish, and promise. The New Testament is the fulfillment of the promise.

Between the birth of Jesus Christ and the end of Revelation, we find a catechism of how Christians are to structure their lives. More important than this, the pages in between contain the crucifixion and resurrection of our Savior. The greatest events of all recorded time are found in this in-between part.

From the first verse in Matthew to the last of Revelation, we learn about relationship with God through the work and sacrifice of Jesus Christ. All the rules we need are contained in this "in-between" section. The events that took us from being lost to being chosen for residence in a heavenly mansion are recorded in the in-between.

What does this mean to us? In our temporal lives, the most important moments are certainly not our birth or death. The days and years in between are what count. Of course, births and deaths are important events. The details of our birth and death will probably be much more significant in the lives of others than to our own. Hopefully, our birth was a significant event to our parents; our death may be so for our children.

What we do with the in-between part is what matters. The love we share, the lessons we teach, the example we set; these create the fragrance of the bouquet of our lives. We did not set our date of birth and seldom do we establish our time of death. We can, however, fill the space between these events with actions and emotions that bless others.

For Christians, there is yet another beginning and end. The day we accept Christ as our Savior marks the start of our journey. The day we return to His presence, whether through our death or His second coming, establishes the end. We will not be judged on either our beginning or end. We are tested, quizzed, and evaluated on the content of our "in-between."

What we do today is of greatest importance. Yesterday is boxed and forgotten. Tomorrow never truly arrives; it just becomes today again.

" 'Some day' doesn't exist, never has, and never will. There is no 'some day.' There's only today." -- Jeff Olson

Wonderful marriages are not built on the glamorous foundation of a wedding day, but the sum of all the shared todays. Are you concentrating on what was or what might be? There is little profit in that. Live fully in your today; it's all you have.

[176]

Shiner and Ace came into our lives and then left again. The story didn't end there. A new beginning was established when we found them on the parched hills of that barren pasture. One day the story will end. When it does, the details of the beginning really won't matter. What does matter is the relationship Shiner and Ace share with us in these in-between days. If I am successful in providing worthy leadership and instruction, they will mix with what each horse brings to the table in terms of his own desires and needs to produce something rich and wonderful.

Each day is a full life, from the birth of morning to the passing away of the day at midnight. The opportunity of each day disappears as the clock strikes twelve and a new day begins. Every time you hear of an unexpected death, you should be reminded that your in-between time is limited. None of us knows when our middle may suddenly become our end. Both humans and horses have accidents or acute medical crises that find a grieving family at day's end that had to say goodbye to a loved one, never anticipating what would happen between that morning and that night.

Regrets are reserved for those who live forever in their yesterdays or their tomorrows. Was your lesson with your horse less than perfect yesterday? Were you less than successful in your walk with the Lord last Tuesday? That mistakes were made isn't the issue. What matters is what you do with your today.

Did you do damage to an important relationship today? Go out today and repair it. Did you fall victim to that one temptation that snares you again and again? Don't let it drag you down today. Yesterday is gone. Today is what matters—this day and every today that will dawn.

[177]

The family of Jesus Christ is being called together. The narrow gate was finally opened by the victory on Calvary and waits to welcome those with a mansion reserved in heaven. Whether or not we arrive and pass through that gate is a product of the relationship we have with Jesus Christ today.

Focus on the in-between time. Concentrate your thoughts and efforts on today.

TOGETHER AGAIN

We began our search for Shiner and Ace to bring the family together. At the time, we were only thinking about Sky's family, bringing home the boys to take their father's now-vacant place at our table.

Shiner and Ace returned home to share a beautiful pasture while regaining their strength and their spirits. Eventually they moved into the barn so I could begin to build on the most rudimentary foundations we had established when they first arrived. Ace and Shiner will soon be ten years old, and it will be a new experience for me to be starting forever relationships with middle-aged horses.

It is time to offer Shiner and Ace a relationship. Will it be in their spirit to accept our offer? If so, then we will be faithful to teach them, to lead them, and to make them a vital part of the family. If not, then they will be semi-retired to the pasture to live out the rest of their lives as beloved pets. If we offer well, the choice made will be entirely theirs.

The past week was one of consistent lessons and interaction between Bo, Shiner, Ace, and me. The work officially began two weeks before Christmas. The boys joined Bo and Copper in the barn right after Thanksgiving, but cold and rain kept me from doing much with them besides adding a few basics and reinforcing what they already knew.

The first few days I did ground work with Bo, Shiner, and Ace. I was doing remedial work with Bo, reminding him of his status as my partner and of all the responsibilities and benefits that come with that lofty position. It took about ten minutes for him to rearrange his pony brain and drop back solidly into place. Our experience is just more proof that solid foundations have very long shelf lives.

Shiner took a bit longer than Bo to engage, and Ace is just interesting. I've ridden Bo and Shiner six of the past seven days. Ace has had little lessons designed to focus his attention on my body language and to move his feet at my direction without a halter or lead rope.

Everyone is making progress.

The big news recently is the change in the relationships among the four geldings themselves. At this point, I don't know where these changes will ultimately lead. We will learn together as my relationship with each horse progresses.

At midmorning recently, I turned each gelding out of the barn in order, beginning from the south and working my way north along their back gates. Ace went first, then Shiner, then Bo, and lastly, Copper.

Ace nurdled around in the short grass at the back of the barn, and Shiner headed directly out into the pasture to nibble bits of brown grass farther away. Horses always nip the grass nearest the barn as close to the ground as their teeth permit. Why they don't just walk a few yards farther to find taller grass, I don't know. However, like most horses, they are wonderfully consistent.

As Bo left his stall, he headed out to the spot where Ace and Shiner were now standing, Shiner still busily

[180]

nibbling grass. When I turned around next, I saw Ace, head high, ears backed, challenging Bo and removing him from the spot. I didn't see the genesis of this exchange, so I don't know if Ace was claiming Shiner or simply claiming his own space.

Wow! I stood there waiting to see what next moves might be made to help me fill in the missing pieces and understand just what communication had taken place between Ace and Bo. Unfortunately, Bo simply turned and walked in a different direction. Ace went back to graze next to Shiner, who hadn't bothered to raise his head once. Peace returned to the pasture.

Why was I glued to the exchange, hoping for more?

The move that Ace made on Bo, for whatever reason, is the equivalent of an autistic child suddenly meeting the eye of another person, locking on, and interacting in a normal manner. Ace initiated a response to a member of his herd rather than simply reacting to an outside stimulus. Whatever he said to Bo had to be quite ordinary for Bo to simply shrug it off and look for a new bit of grass. This is a huge breakthrough of some kind, but I don't know what kind quite yet.

As the day progressed, I went out to clean the barn before calling the geldings back to get saddled and ready for lessons. They did not come immediately. Usually when the horses see me near the barn, they head on over for dinner, attention, or access to their houses.

I didn't call them. I stopped picking manure out of the dirt and shavings. I leaned on the handle of my cleaning fork and watched. Fascinating. I felt almost like I was on safari in the darkest parts of Africa, watching the native animals go about their routines in ways natural to them but unknown to man.

Bo and Shiner were playing together as if they were colts still pastured with their mothers, romping, frolicking, and running with gleeful, equine abandon. Shiner and Bo were running, Shiner following close to Bo's hip as they sailed over the grass together. For a reason known only to them, Bo and Shiner would stop, engage each other face to face, and then Shiner would tear out again, this time with Bo bringing up the rear.

Amazing. They were acting like brothers. I almost choked up, recognizing that bonds of trust, familiarity, and *herdship* were forming right before my eyes.

What a gift! But what happened next elevated the occasion to an even higher level. Bo and Ace began to play with each other. Bo and Ace were playing nibble-face, standing hoof to hoof, sparring with each other using their muzzles and necks. When horses play like this, neither one backs off; it is the equivalent of thumb wrestling among people. The thumbs are the horse's faces, their necks the hands and wrist. The rest of the body doesn't enter into play.

I was tempted to leave the boys out in pasture to play. By the time the one-on-one games ended, all four geldings were leaping, turning, running, and joyfully experiencing recess on a beautiful winter afternoon in the sun. This was a first.

It seemed that school was not going to be cancelled for the day, however. When I finished picking the barn and putting fresh shavings in the stalls, I looked back to the pasture and saw Bo and Copper off in one area and Shiner and Ace in another. It appears recess was over. I called them in. They came. Lessons began again.

It has only been a few months since we were reunited with Shiner and Ace, yet it seems in some ways as if they never left. Shiner is quickly stepping up to the relationship plate. He is responsive and seems to value our time together.

Ace, on the other hand, is going to take time to understand. Is he the way he is because he is unable or unwilling? It really doesn't matter at the moment. The fix is the same and he isn't going anywhere. Ace and Shiner are home to stay.

He Came Looking for Me

REDEEMED

"The groom wasn't pleased to see the horse dealer bring a horse for trial who had blemished knees. His arm was twisted and he relented to at least give the big black horse a try.

As Joe Green groomed the new horse for the first time he noticed similarities to the Black Beauty of his youth, the horse he nearly killed out of ignorance; his early mistress' most beloved horse until ill health caused her husband to liquidate home and stables.

Further inspection confirmed that this new horse, with evidence of much bad history to mix with the fine of his own memory, was indeed the exceptional Black Beauty. All concerns of soundness issues disappeared, replaced completely with nothing but concern for Beauty's care." -- Black Beauty: The Autobiography of a Horse

Joe Green overlooked the experience and expertise he used to evaluate horses when he realized that the noble creature who looked into his eyes was Black Beauty. Any thoughts of should and should not immediately disappeared. Not only was the horse before him worth the effort and cost to save him, but the gift of a new beginning with Beauty could absolve him of the mistake he made so many years before. What a perfect picture of the fruit of grace.

[185]

Jesus did not die for any flock. He died for His flock. He will not take home a full complement of random souls when he returns. He will take home each and every person whose name is on that bloodstained list and in His heart.

We went looking for Shiner and Ace. We found them and brought them home at the precise moment they needed to be redeemed. We paid the meager price necessary to make them fully ours.

"After this it was quite decided to keep me and call me by my old name of 'Black Beauty.'...My ladies have promised that I shall never be sold, and so I have nothing to fear; and here my story ends. My troubles are over, and I am at home; and often before I am quite awake, I fancy I am still in the orchard at Birtwick standing with my old friends under the apple tree."

-- Black Beauty: The Autobiography of a Horse

Jesus went looking for me. He has redeemed me and will bring me home at the precise time I need to be found. He paid the ultimate price necessary to make me fully His.

If you haven't been found just yet, remember Ace and Shiner. Behind the scenes, invisible to your natural eyes, Jesus is looking for you and won't stop until you are home with Him. He will find you and bring you home at exactly the right moment. The price was paid on Calvary to make you solely His.

None other can claim you, not in this world or beyond. By grace and victory, you have been redeemed.

It is personal.

The Round Up

God's amazing grace blesses me with a relationship to horses that lets me live out the lessons I am meant to both learn and to teach. One of the purposes of this book, as well as *Amazing Grays, Amazing Grace*, is to try and bring the family of God together. The time has come to round up the strays.

He Came Looking for Me has a three-fold message:

1. Jesus Christ is a personal savior. He doesn't seek to meet some quota for salvation. He seeks each of us by name. None other will do.

2. We are saved by grace. The only thing strong enough, big enough, everlasting enough, to bridge the distance between heaven and earth is the grace of God. Grace is ours. The battles we fight are really just skirmishes that persist because the loser has yet to concede the war. The truth, however, is that the war is over. Jesus Christ is King of Kings. Satan has been defeated. The work is done; it is complete. When Christ spoke, "It is finished" on Calvary, He meant it literally. The war is over. All we need do is claim the victory that is already ours.

3. In this time of spiritual activity, the enemy wants us to think that there are still meaningful battles to fight that will still have an effect upon the ultimate outcome of the war. We are blessed to know that no such meaningful battles remain.

[187]

It is time, however, for the children of God to begin coming together. The flock is being assembled. Just as Ace and Shiner came home, all in God's family are being called in. Listen for the Shepherd's voice. He is calling you by name.

We went looking for Ace and Shiner as individuals. God allowed us to find them at the very time they most needed to be rescued. You'll never convince me that this was anything other than a divine appointment.

What was it that forged the links in the chain of events from the first tiny little thought Baber and I shared about missing Sky to driving through our front gate with both of his sons in the trailer behind us? Grace.

There is a narrow gate somewhere before us. It is the only entrance to home, to heaven. When Ace and Shiner entered through our gate, they passed through the one and only gate that for them led to heaven and their home pasture.

And one day the entire family will be reunited— through the narrow gate that opens to our home pasture beyond.

NEW YEAR, NEW LIFE

The drifted snow in the pasture comes up to my knees as I walk the last few paces to the barn. It's been a long time since it was hot. Unlike we horses, people seem to keep track of years and not just seasons, and I know a new year just began.

Ace and I played out in the snow this morning, just messing around like brothers, enjoying ourselves until Baber came out with our breakfast. Truth be told, we're not really that hungry, as our feeder was loaded with sweet-smelling hay last night.

Sally and the donkey came over for a brief visit earlier. We talked across the fence for a bit before she decided to take her thirty-year-old body back in to the stall on her side of the barn. It's still snowing, but not as much as it was. I've taken to spending a lot of time under our roof. From my cozy vantage point, I have a view of our pasture and the neighbor's cows that lets me keep up with their comings and goings, the new calves, and I can also see if the barn horses come out today.

Bo, Swizzle, Asti, Copper, Ace, and I take turns spending time in the big barn and being out here in the smaller barn and pasture. Ace and I were in the big barn for quite a while as Lynn was teaching us lessons. Now we're free to be outside whenever we want to or inside whenever

[189]

we want to. In the big barn, we spent some time out each day after our lessons and slept inside.

I have discovered that I stay nice and warm if I don't get wet. Not too long ago, there was a long rainy time—and cold! People don't seem to understand that our thick winter coats are like blankets of ice when they get wet in winter. But Lynn and Baber brought out new, wool-lined, waterproof blankets for Ace, Sally, and me. Our roof next to the barn was also made much larger, and I haven't shivered even once.

We always knew that you could get into the barn from under our shade, but the door only opened when Baber was bringing us breakfast or dinner. I waited for him there every day. Mealtimes are so regular that Ace and I pretty much know when the door will open and the buckets will be coming through. Every once in a while, I go to the door and put my muzzle up to the place between the top of the door and the eave to check on any activity inside. After all, it's only polite to be there, ready, when meals are served.

After Ace and I had been here for a while, our appetites returned and we started feeling hungry again. Once we started looking for more to eat, we rushed to the feeders as soon as there was food. Lynn showed us that we were not behaving well and we learned to have better manners. Now, since we are never without something to nibble on, we just try hard to let our people know how happy we are to see them.

A Door Opens

Just after the cold season started, the door to the barn opened and has stayed open ever since. Ace and I have a large stall with shavings to lie in whenever we want. We can see Sally and the donkey in their stall just a few yards away on the other side of the barn aisle.

I love the barn. Unless I am in the mood to go looking for a choice, green blade of winter grass, I like to stand in the stall, my head sticking out, watching my neighborhood.

Ace and I have discovered the power nap. We used to take quick naps on our feet, never able to relax or get really comfortable in the sun or bad weather. Now that we have our own tree, a big covered area next the barn, and a roomy stall, we always have shelter. On nice days, we have a spot on the fence where we lie down together like puppies and sleep for the longest time.

I am reminded of our home pasture, all those years ago when Ace and I could nap without worries, our mothers watching over us. Now that I think about it, we sleep without worries now. Our winter coats are thick and lustrous, and we always have food and clean water.

Even when we aren't in the big barn, we see Lynn and Baber several times a day when they come to visit us or work around our place. There is always a greeting for us, and we discovered the special places in the fences a long time ago.

Our pasture has wonderful places along the fence where we get pets and carrots. And I have discovered how nice it feels to have the spot between my eyes softly rubbed.

"Shiner!"

Thanks for the visit, but I've gotta go. Lynn is calling me. My name is Shiner, and this is my home pasture.

Shiner and Lynn

EPILOGUE: THE ONE

He pulled his cap down firmly over his brow. With one last push, he swung the narrow gate open on sturdy but very rusty hinges. The gate had been closed a long, long time.

For longer than any man could remember, no one had been able to open this gate. Men of every type, size, and manner had tried. The gate had been rammed, jimmied, set ablaze, and the attempts to bypass it far too many to count. Every attempt ended the same; the gate remained shut and no one gained entrance. Yet there it was, standing wide open as if in expectation.

Once he passed through from that side to this, he took precise care to settle the gate against the solid wall that separated inside from outside. The only passage through the wall was this single, tiny gate. Ancient hasps engaged, insuring that the gate could not close again. This gate would not be closed again until he brought the last one home.

Turning his back to the gate, his face set in purpose, he began walking. In his pocket was a tattered, hand-written list. Written on the list were the names of each one he would bring home.

With no witness other than the gate itself, the man set out to finish the journey he had begun so very long ago.

He is looking for me.

HE CAME LOOKING FOR ME

DISCUSSION AND STUDY SECTION:

Making the Message Personal

This section includes suggested questions and topics designed to promote conversation and discussion about the messages of *He Came Looking for Me*. Book clubs, Bible studies, families and horse buddies can sit together and talk about how their own experiences compare to Shiner's.

Work through the questions in chapter order or simply pick one that starts you thinking...

The Search Begins

1. Have you ever had the feeling there was something missing in your life but had no idea what it could be?

2. We have all mourned lost relationships. What were the circumstances of losing one of your meaningful relationships? Could anything have saved it?

3. If you encountered Jesus in His mortal form, what would be your first reaction? How would you explain a Person both human and divine to a friend?

4. Is there really such a thing as a coincidence? Do miracles still exist?

Coming Home

1. We know that "all things work together for the good" of God's children [Romans 8:28]. What door has

been closed in your life? Did another open? How might this story help you process previous losses or failures?

2. Lynn and Baber saw the hand of God at work in the return of Ace and Shiner. Have you witnessed God working in real time in your own life? Looking back, is there something you used to believe was a simple coincidence that was really a deliberate act of God?

3. What commonality is there between Ace's itch and people trying to deal with addictions? What clues in the behavior of someone you know indicate that an intervention might be necessary?

It is Personal

1. The author believes that the amount of spiritual activity in the world is increasing at breakneck speed; some good and some evil. Do you share the conviction that the family of God is being called together? Why or why not? List some examples.

2. The personal nature of Jesus' commitment to us is hard to define or even comprehend. Take a moment and put yourself at the foot of the Cross and "watch" as your name slowly appears on the list. See each letter of your name form, made visible only by the presence of His blood. In one sentence, how could you share the experience with someone who needs to know the truth of God's promises?

3. Before coming home, Shiner spent each day in a dry barren pasture without hope and waiting for a merciful end to his suffering. Have you ever been there? What pulled you back? What made you care again? Where did hope come from?

Reflection

1. Have you ever had a child or employee behave in a rude or demanding way to you? What did you do? How would you respond if your child said, "Hurry up and do what I want"? What if it was a student - or even your dog?

2. Both parents and pet owners occasionally use physical intervention on their kids and critters. Give examples of the appropriate use of physical intervention and others that are not. Have you ever witnessed abuse caused by frustration or anger? Did you react or remain silent?

3. What is the status of each of your relationship savings accounts? Do you have healthy balances or are you overdrawn? How will you get out of relationship red and back to the black for your overdrawn accounts?

4. When did you last experience a relationship conflict or made a promise you didn't want to keep? What did you do? Did you add to the relationship savings account? How do you think God feels when we break a commitment to Him?

Commitment

1. What has been the impact on society by the changing and blurring roles of men, women, and children? Do these changes support or undermine God's plan as outlined in Scripture? How?

2. Are the presents you give at Christmas or birthdays true gifts as defined by the author? Does the Bible support the idea of gifts as a transaction or as a one-way gesture?

3. What gifts or talents are you naturally blessed with? Do you make the best use of them or simply enjoy them? When should you pursue a gift and when should you offer it to the Lord as a sacrifice of praise?

Undaunted

1. Do you know anyone who is living an undaunted (truly victorious) life? Is that person just silly or has he or she solved some mystery? What do you think the secret might be?

2. What in your life is still problematic? Is there any circumstance where you just cannot say, "I'm good with that"? What is the basis for your concern? What could bring you peace? Is there a choice to be made?

3. What lesson do we teach others when we fret and worry? Is this behavior consistent with a relationship with Jesus Christ?

Faith - Hope - Love

1. What is your definition of faith?

2. The author suggests that the presence of fear always indicates a lack of faith. Do your children know any fear? As a parent are you worthy of your children's faith? Are you worthy of the faith your pet has in you? Is there any circumstance that makes fear a reasonable option?

3. Do you agree with the author's presentation of faith, hope, and love? Is it supported scripturally? What other verses in the Bible speak to faith, hope, and love?

Ace and Tantrums

1. How is Ace's poor behavior similar to a human tantrum? Are they rooted in the same cause?

2. The author suggests that Ace's issue isn't one of making noise at feeding time, and that his behavior is really a symptom of something deeper. What is the problem and what is the proposed solution?

Turning Up the Flame

1. How do you define "fear of God"? How does the author illustrate such fear in her relationship with the misbehaving Ace?

2. What similarities exist in bringing up children and coaching top-notch athletes using the methods Lynn applied in Ace's lessons?

3. In your opinion, is there any truth that some folks are homeless by preference? Does Ace remind you of anyone you have met? Who and why?

Leadership

1. Give an example from the Bible where God was "fearful" on purpose. What was His goal? Was the object of His action one of His children or an unbeliever?

2. The author believes that proper authority and leadership creates a strong chain that produces faith that overcomes fear. How does the failure of leadership at home weaken the family?

3. Describe three observable results of failed leadership.

Temptation

1. Do dreams really bring messages from God? What is your personal experience?

2. When your child, your student, or your pet becomes agitated, nervous, or fearful, how can you help him or her return to a "state of grace"? How does God do it for us?

3. What allowed Lynn to restore Shiner to his own place of obedience, content, and happiness in a matter of ninety seconds? How could the same concept be applied in human relationships?

4. Where are you most vulnerable to temptation? Did you learn anything from the author's experience? Can you identify a pattern in your own history of failure?

Never Too Late

1. Put yourself in the place of the vineyard worker: when were you offered employment? What were the circumstances of your acceptance or rejection?

2. Recall your own definition of faith. Have you ever asked God, "Do you think you can make me?" What did Shiner learn?

New Year, New Life

1. Shiner has been made a new creation by relationship with Lynn. He is enjoying the benefits of a new life restored to his home pasture. His story is one of hope, redemption, and grace. Describe how grace has been made manifest in your new life in Jesus Christ.

2. Place yourself in Shiner's position as he gives us his final thought in his story. What is your circumstance and what voice do you hear? Are you found? Is every need met? What is the status of your faith today?

3. Shiner shared his experience with you - have you shared yours with someone else?

ABOUT THE AUTHOR

A former business consultant and motivational speaker, Christian writer Lynn Baber exchanged the board room for the barn at the end of the 1980's. Her success as an equine professional includes achievement as a World and National Champion horse breeder and trainer, judge, Certified Equine Appraiser, and expert witness.

The primary message of Lynn's work is "Faith over Fear." She openly shares lessons learned from personal experience with domestic violence, hopelessness, serious family illness, failure, perseverance, and success. Lynn teaches the principles of being a worthy leader and the pursuit of true fearlessness in today's world.

Lynn says the messages she delivered as a motivational speaker were absolutely correct, but today she knows where these principles are found in the Bible. Whether shared in print, in person, or in the round pen working with troubled horses, the message will always be God's faithfulness and grace.

Living her dream in Weatherford, Texas, Lynn and her husband Baber (Larry) share the barn with their horses, dogs, cats and goats. She says, "It took me more than three decades of success to finally live in the barn."

Other titles by Lynn Baber:

Rapture and Revelation - Welcome to the End Time, (2012)

The King is coming. This is the End Time and a choice must be made between God and Not God. Why do you believe what you believe? Many Christians have been shocked to discover that the "jesus" they know is not the Son of God. Simple, direct, with extensive citations of the scriptures that support the message.

Amazing Grays, Amazing Grace - Pursuing relationship with God, horses, and one another (2010, 2013)

"Amazing Grays" is a scripturally based master class in worthy leadership using the relationship between human and horse as a mirror of that between God and man. Packed with concepts and true illustrations ranging from discipline to distraction, communication to commitment, and domination to Grace. Each chapter begins with a scripture then brings it to life in the arena or round pen of life.

The Art of Being Foolish Proof: the best kept customer service secret, (1989)

Contact information:

www.AmazingGraysMinistry.com
lynn@amazinggraysministry.com

AMAZING GRAYS, AMAZING GRACE

Pursuing relationship with God,
horses, and one another

LYNN BABER

Amazing Grays, Amazing Grace

© Lynn Baber 2010, 2013 , all rights reserved

ISBN # - 978-1-938836-03-9

Published by Ark Press

Amazing Grays Ministry.

PO Box 187

Weatherford, TX 76086

AMAZING GRAYS, AMAZING GRACE

INTRODUCTION

The day is unveiled as the morning sun slowly begins to rise above the black-green trees and deep-purple hills, each new angle of sunlight creating an original canvas upon which God's artwork appears to those who are awake to behold its glory. As dawn progresses, trees take on more distinct form, and the buildings and structures on the hills rise out of a flat landscape as if elevated from below.

Grass becomes a luxurious carpet of vibrant green as new sunlight reflects through droplets of morning dew. Vague forms of horses grazing contentedly become illuminated as the solar spotlight brings their once ghostly images into sharply focused view, allowing me to identify each one in turn. My eyes search for confirmation that my little herd has made it safely through another night. I see the tall, black mare, the powerful dun, and my two grays. All is well.

This is a day that the Lord has made; let us rejoice and be glad in it. God is ever faithful, each morning bringing new life and opportunity to His family. I rested well last night, safe in the assurance that though I slept, He was awake and watching over me. With dawn, the responsibility for my horses passes from God to me, and I will be faithful to them until night returns and I pass the watch back to heaven.

Have you noticed how birds seem to sing with special joy in springtime? Their music accompanies my study as I pause again to look through my east window to the horses grazing beyond, grateful for yet another opportunity to walk with the Lord. My greatest blessing is being a child of God, knowing that He loves me beyond my capacity to comprehend. How can humans possibly grasp the unknowable truths of a relationship with God and with our Savior, Jesus Christ? What could possibly bridge the distance between heaven and earth and allow mere mortals a glimpse of eternity? It is grace.

The Holy Spirit gives each of God's children a unique context that allows us to build a personal relationship with Him. For me, that context is horses. Twenty years training horses was my preparatory school, providing the key I needed to finally grasp what were previously only vague elements of my pursuit of relationship with God. The key to my relationship with God was provided by my amazing grays, Bo and Swizzle. I chose them, and they chose me. Working through my daily lessons with the Holy Spirit allows me to direct and deepen the bond I share with my grays, just as working with horses blesses me with a greater understanding of the absolute truth and promise of God's Word.

The secret of life is relationship with God. The important question is not how, why, where, or when; the important question is "Who?" This book is a collection of concepts and stories, an opportunity to learn how horses allow us to find closer relationships with God. Woven into the fabric of the message is love, correction, wonderment, obedience, accountability, success, failure, birth, and death. But the heartbeat that gives each life is a relationship with the Lord.

Are you pursuing a right relationship to God? As a child of God, *Amazing Grays, Amazing Grace* will help you learn to communicate with the Spirit and experience correction and trial as your habit of task slowly changes to a habit of obedience. As your training progresses, you will begin to see the possibilities of relationship with the Lord that were but ghostly images in a flat landscape. Prepare for the dawn and experience the blessing that a relationship with God brings to your other relationships. Learning to abandon to God will teach you how to be a better parent, teacher, friend, minister, leader, and horse owner.

God has chosen you to be his child.

Praise be to the God and Father of our Lord Jesus Christ, who has blessed us in the heavenly realms with every spiritual blessing in Christ. For He chose us in Him before the creation of the world to be holy and blameless in his sight. In love He predestined us to be adopted as His sons through Jesus Christ, in accordance with his pleasure and will—to the praise of His glorious grace, which He has freely given us in the One He loves.

And you were also included in Christ when you heard the word of truth, the gospel of your salvation. Having believed, you were marked in Him with a seal, the promised Holy Spirit, who is a deposit guaranteeing our inheritance until the redemption of those who are God's possession—to the praise of His glory.

- Ephesians 1:3–6, 13–14

Amazing grace, how sweet is the sound of my grays as they snuffle contentedly in their stalls, secure in the knowledge that I watch over them as He watches over me.

Lynn and Bo

Rapture

And

Revelation

Welcome to the End Time

Lynn Baber

Lynn Baber's new book, *Rapture and Revelation*, has not been written for the reader who wishes to have his or her ears tickled. There are plenty of Christian books and e-books catering for that, but not this one. It is a book-study offering simple truth about the times we're living in, but it's also a challenging book, leaving no room for the reader to express anything but "yes" or "no" for their answers and decisions. No room for fence-sitters!

- Roger Williams, Australian radio broadcaster and blogger

Rapture and Revelation

ISBN 978-1-938836-02-2

INTRODUCTION

"Now this I say, brethren, that flesh and blood cannot inherit the kingdom of God; nor does corruption inherit incorruption. Behold, I tell you a mystery: We shall not all sleep, but we shall all be changed— "

- 1 Corinthians 15:50-51

Welcome to the End Time.

Rapture and Revelation will not tell you what to believe, but will ask you to be honest about *why* you believe *what* you do. This old world is rapidly aging as fires, floods, droughts, earthquakes, and storms ravage every continent. The clock of human history is quickly running down as nations, economies, and religions are either at war with one another or ready to implode upon themselves.

There is an absolute need for messages that offer the simple truth about the times we live in. Trust is something you remember from the good old days, not something you can teach your children today by pointing out a politician, doctor, news anchor, minister, or teacher. Watch the news long enough and you'll have ample reason to distrust all of the above. The absence of trust is the beginning of fear.

False teaching is the greatest hazard for today's Christians. How do you know that many of your core beliefs are not the result of false teaching that originated in false prophecy? *Rapture and Revelation* will challenge you to examine what you believe and compare it to the source - God's Word.

"Beloved, do not believe every spirit, but test the spirits, whether they are of God; because many false prophets have gone out into the world. And this is the spirit of the Antichrist, which you have heard was coming, and is now already in the world."

- 1 John 4:1, 3

One choice eclipses all others, the choice between God and Not God. This sounds like an easy choice, but don't be deceived. Most Christians would probably say, "Of course I choose God." Unfortunately, many of them would be wrong.

Our society is divided on almost every topic from ecology to abortion. If there is one thing most people might agree upon it would be that there is no such thing as absolute truth.

Do you believe that anything is absolutely true or right in all instances and circumstances without exception? What would that one thing be?

Do you believe that the Bible is the inerrant and inspired Word of God and that every single verse is true?

Are you sure you know what I mean by 'Bible'? Whether or not you participate in the Rapture may depend upon knowing the difference between what five familiar words *used* to mean and what they mean today.

These five words no longer have a common definition which makes speaking or debating issues of politics, culture, or faith a real mess. In fact, it isn't even possible to define these words unless you first resolve the issue of whether or not absolutes exist.

- God
- Jesus
- Christian
- Grace
- Antichrist

There are as many unique relationships with God as there are humans. Just as every parent-child relationship is different so is the experience of every child of the King of Kings who pursues right relationship with Him. The experience of any friend, pastor, teacher, or writer will not be the same as yours. Yours will not be the same as mine. We are children of the same true God but no two will ever walk an identical path of sanctification. *Rapture and Revelation* is a tool for your use, intended to enlighten and support you as you persevere with all in the family of Christ.

Are you sure you know ***why*** you believe ***what*** you believe?

Are you certain you define God the same way your friends do? Are the lessons about tolerance and spirituality taught in public schools consistent with God's Word or some other gospel that has nothing to do with Jesus of Nazareth? Does your pastor preach the words of the apostles or those approved by a more progressive theology? If you don't know exactly how simple words like Jesus, Christian, and Grace are used, how will you know if what you hear is true or false?

"Not everyone who says to Me, 'Lord, Lord,' shall enter the kingdom of heaven, but he who does the will of My Father in heaven. Many will say to Me in that day, 'Lord, Lord, have we not prophesied in Your name, cast out demons in Your name, and done many wonders in Your name?' And then I will declare to them, 'I never knew you; depart from Me, you who practice lawlessness!' " - Matthew 7:21-24

How can you be certain that the Jesus you know is the One who needs to know you? Of course, some popular Christian denominations would assure you it doesn't really matter and that all will be well. They're wrong.

Bible scholarship is simply that -- the study of a book titled *The Bible*. Every academic who studies the words in that book is free to teach whatever opinion he or she draws from the exercise - and they do. The best, brightest, and most credentialed academics across twenty centuries do not agree on what the Bible says. I'm not suggesting I belong among those scholars. I'm just a regular person tapped by God to serve the family of Christ. The ultimate responsibility to "rightly divide" the Word of God [2 Timothy 2:15] is yours alone.

This is the End Time. Perhaps you will see Jesus Christ today. But even if the Rapture does not occur in your natural lifetime, living in harmony, peace, and joy with God will bless you every day until you finally pass into immortality.

How do I know this is the End Time? The morning of March 11, 2011 changed my life forever.